Drama
WITHIN
English

A collection of drama pieces for KS3

Drama pieces by Keith West
Lesson notes by Nichola Knight
and Polly Peters

Evans Brothers Limited

Published by Evans Brothers Limited
2A Portman Mansions
Chiltern Street
London
W1U 6NR

British Library Cataloguing
Data
West, Keith
Drama within English
1.Drama – History and criticism - Juvenile literature
2.Acting - Juvenile literature
I.Title
809.2

ISBN 0237523868

Editor: Louise John
Design: Neil Sayer
Production: Jenny Mulvanny

ISBN 0 237 52386 8

Printed in Malta

Drama WITHIN English

A collection of drama pieces for KS3

Contents

Introduction

Drama is an integral part of teaching English and the Framework for English and the revised National Curriculum for English place a high emphasis on drama at Key Stage 3. Both of these documents provide a number of detailed drama objectives for each year group and this book is designed to help teachers, specialist and non-specialist alike, make links between these drama objectives and other demands within English. Drama, as a teaching tool, will allow pupils to raise their own standards in English and literacy and will generally build confidence.

Drama Within English is aimed at all ability groups at Key Stage 3. The book provides an overview of the many different aspects of drama ... from monologues to the absurd, using a range of learning styles, and allows pupils to enjoy practising drama techniques.

The individual scripts in the book can be photocopied for class use. The follow-up activities within the lesson notes are designd to offer a range of responses to these scripts. They are intended primarily for the teacher's use, but are actually addressed to the pupil. This means that they can be read out verbatim by the teacher preparing the lesson, ruling out the need for interpretation and further investigation. They can also be made into OHP transparencies or photocopied for pupils to refer to when completing the activities.

All of the activities are class-based. There are three suggested responses to each script. Firstly, a 'seated' response. Pupils remain at their desks but are instructed in activities, which can be used for speaking and listening assessments. Secondly, an 'active' response. This is a more specifically drama-orientated response as it offers suggestions for an 'on-their-feet-pens-down-no-desks' dramatic exploration of ideas linked to the texts. And, finally, a written response is offered.

Basic Drama Techniques

The following section contains descriptions for the teacher of some of the best-used basic drama techniques. These descriptions are intended primarily for the English teacher who is uninitiated in using drama in a classroom setting. They are designed to encourage active and participatory drama opportunities.

Improvisation

Improvisation is, at its most basic level, a game of 'let's pretend'. It is spontaneous action in which individuals enact roles in order to explore situations, exercise choice, analyse responses and to make decisions. It can be used to free a pupil's imagination within a structured activity where the imagination is focused towards a particular task.

Improvisation in either pairs or groups requires the individual to use very direct skills of communication. In order to enter into a 'let's pretend' situation of suspended disbelief, there are complex social exchanges occurring. Each individual is encouraged to develop her/his ability to negotiate, to share, to give and take, to co-operate and to communicate. During the act of improvising or 'pretending', each person has the chance to make unforced verbal contribution, to listen to others' ideas, to share opinions, to show sensitivity to the text and to each other and to learn the ensemble skill of being equally important in a group situation. Above all, improvisation offers great opportunity for confidence-building.

Although it requires a spontaneous reaction, constructive improvisation does not happen spontaneously. The best way to set it up is to establish firm ground rules initially about the way in which pupils should work together. This includes making rules about:

- respecting everyone's ideas
- including everyone
- making constructive criticism
- helping each other
- not blocking ideas

For the purposes of response to a text during an English lesson, improvisation is more about the process rather than achieving perfect results. It should be regarded by pupils as work in progress – demanding an immediate response to a particular situation, enabling the development and practice of various skills. You may want to plan beforehand how to group pupils for the most effective group dynamics (see Group Work).

Freeze-frame

Also known as 'tableau', 'snapshot' or 'still-life'. The use of freeze-frame involves asking pupils to create a group picture which tells a moment from a story. An effective freeze-frame should be created thoughtfully and deliberately, rather than instantly. Pupils should be instructed to consider how the following elements combine to communicate an impression to an onlooker:

- grouping
- gestures
- posture
- facial expressions
- spatial expression of group members
- focal point

When working with freeze-frames it is useful to use a count-down from five to one for getting each frozen picture into position. If pupils are working to present more than one freeze-frame in succesion, then using a count-down between each picture gives them time to get into their final position for the count of 'one'. Allow time for the rest of the class to evaluate the freeze-frames presented. In particular, they should be encouraged to look for the focal point of each picture and to comment on how specific elements combine to tell a story.

Group Work

Instructing pupils to 'Get into groups of four' can work well with a motivated, responsive class. In a less enthusiastic class, it can take fifteen minutes to achieve this and can be combined with a mixture of apathy, sulks and even conflict! As an alternative, you can use numbering to create random groups. This has the advantage, when used frequently, of getting every pupil in the class used to working closely with every other pupil in it.

For a class of 30 that you may wish to divide into groups of five, number pupils from one to six, then repeat this until every pupil has a number. Instruct the 'ones' to stand together and then the 'twos', and so on so that groups are instantly created. Another way of random grouping is to play 'mingle and grab', where the pupils are instructed to walk around each other. The teacher shouts a number and pupils instantly have to form a group of that size from the people nearest to them. Play this several times with different numbers and end with a number for the size of the group you want. A third alternative is to work out the groups on paper beforehand to allow for some friendship grouping, but also to avoid unconstructive dynamics between individuals. This also allows for inclusion of pupils who may otherwise be treated as loners.

Monologues

A monologue is a long speech made by one character. The character is usually speaking directly to the audience.

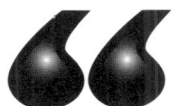

Future Clone Girl

A girl walks on stage, holding a notebook, and speaks earnestly to the audience.

You wouldn't believe how like my mother I am. She's dead, though. She died long before I was born. Can you believe that? Extraordinary, but true. In a way, she wasn't just my mum, she was me too, or rather, I am her. (*pause*) Yes, I know, I speak in riddles, but you will understand. Just hear me out.

If my mother died before I was born, how did I get here? Biotechnology – there's a clue! Who has brought me up? My stepparents have – they were carefully selected by my mother and given very precise instructions on how to look after me. After all, even before I was born, my mother knew me better than I know myself yet. You see, I am a clone of my mother. I am my mother, my mother is me.

Mum had a rotten childhood and she was determined I wouldn't suffer in the way that she had. She was a very imaginative child, lived in a world of her own a lot of the time, but her parents disapproved of her mind games. They were simple, hard-working people who had no time for dreamers. They gave her a hard time. And school was no better. The other children taunted her, bullied her even. The teachers tried their best to strangle her imagination – what chance was there for her in needlework or science or maths, after all? So Mum decided I wouldn't have to go to school. My imagination is allowed to run riot, it is indulged so that I might reach my full potential.

If I am my mum, and she was very imaginative – she even had some science-fiction books published – why do I find it so difficult to think like she did? Why can't I write like she did? I should be able to write a bestseller, given all the advantages I've had. But I can't think of a single storyline. Why? (*pause*) Yes, I suppose that's it. My clone mother made one big mistake. She protected me in advance from life's experiences, from the ups and downs, the fun and the fights. In short – I've nothing to write about!

She throws the notebook down in disgust and storms off.

Lesson Notes

Seated

In pairs

Prepare a spoken performance of the text, with each person speaking alternate paragraphs. Imagine that this piece will be performed on radio and that the reason for having two voices is to suggest to the listeners that the clone girl is divided into two people: herself and her mother. Concentrate on the pace you use to speak the lines. Try varying whether you are speaking quickly or slowly. Comment on what the effect is (e.g. speaking slowly makes it sound dreamier and also allows for more dramatic emphasis of specific lines. Speaking quickly is more consistent with the chain of chatter from a young girl and enlivens the delivery.)

You could also make an audio tape of the finished performance. At the end, add comments about yourselves as performers – what decisions you made about how to perform it and what effect you wanted these decisions to have on the audience.

Active

In pairs

Read through the script several times together, taking it in turns to read alternate paragraphs. Put the scripts down and, without looking at them, question each other on how much you remember of what the girl says. Check what you have recalled against the script one more time. Now, work together to prepare an improvised performance based closely on the script. Concentrate particularly on the visual effect you want to create. While one person speaks, the other person will mime (to suggest that Clone Girl is divided into two people). You can either have:

- one person doing all the speaking with the other miming throughout. This works well if the person speaking the story stays fairly still and the person miming performs suitable actions. Alternatively, the person speaking can also perform appropriate movements, which are copied exactly by the other performer as though they are a mirror image or shadow.
- both performers speaking alternate improvised sections. While one speaks, the other moves and vice versa.

Written

Write a research project on cloning using non-fiction resources, or construct an argument either for, or against, scientific cloning.

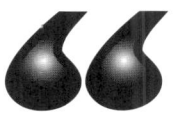

Fugitive

A furtive-looking character sneaks on stage and checks no one is following. As the fugitive speaks, he/she struggles to control tears of despair.

When they poured across the border like a swarm of locusts, we thought we could repel them, push them back. But their tanks and their weapons were too many. They soon took away our freedom. Freedom! Dad thought he would fight for freedom and perhaps he finally found it – in his death. Then the enemy came. I could hear the crunch their boots made on the gravel path. They took Mum away and… and I hid like a coward in the space under the stairs.

One fog-filled frosty morning I made it from the village to the woods. You can disappear in the fog, become a shadow. The woods are alive with the dispossessed, the orphans, the would-be freedom fighters and those who still believe in dreams.

The mountains take the real battlers, the desperados, those that will win our country back for us! Through the trees the wind of change is blowing and at night the false owls hoot their signals. There is movement in the woods – a long procession moves slowly, silently towards the mountains.

The fugitive points out the movement of people.

There are others, too. The marching women who clutch their crying babies. The white-bearded old men who shuffle like ghosts towards Hades. All walk towards the border, their bellies empty, their feet blistered, begging for freedom's help. The grim-faced children clutching broken toys and empty water bottles. Behind and beside them are the hated enemy, driving these, my people, away from their burning villages, their destroyed homes. Yet, we will be avenged.

The fugitive points to the audience.

One day, you will join me. One day, the cry of freedom will be on your lips. For I am the representative of every nation who is invaded by evil and greed – invaded by those who believe might is right, invaded by those who do not want peace. Like shadows you will rise and heed the call. You will find me, and those like me, in the mountains.

There is the sound of gunshots off-stage.

I must go. They search for me and I must disappear. I must melt away like snow on a spring morning.

The fugitive sneaks off-stage.

Lesson Notes

Seated

In groups   Discuss and brainstorm the following:
- What the word 'freedom' means to you now. Consider your age group, your culture, your community and life in Britain.
- What the word 'freedom' seems to mean to the fugitive in this monologue.
- Discuss why this piece is not placed in a specific time or country. Suggest reasons for this.

Active

In groups   Devise one or more tableaux (freeze-frames) to depict what is being described in each paragraph. Perform with one person speaking the monologue while others perform the sequence of freeze-frames.

Written

Write a diary based on what happened to Mum and Dad. Consider the following:
- What events led up to the exodus across the border?
- Which were the most important possessions to take with you?
- What time of day was it?
- How did you get from the village to the woods?
- Did you need any special clothing or equipment?

Duologues

A duologue is a conversation between two characters.

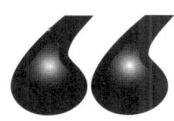 ## Lady Macbeth Talks to her Doctor

Lady Macbeth is speaking to her doctor.

Lady Macbeth: You know I sleep walk, doctor?

Doctor: Yes, your majesty.

Lady Macbeth: And do I talk in my sleep?

Doctor: (*quickly*) Yes, your majesty, some nights you talk in your sleep.

(*silence*)

Lady Macbeth: Ah, you know too much. But what does it matter? What does anything matter now? (*lightly*) I always wanted to be queen, (*with bitterness*) but now I am queen, it's like ashes in my mouth.

Doctor: (*nervous*) I have to attend my other patients, your majesty. If you will excuse me…

Lady Macbeth: (*interrupting*) We were happy, the Thane of Glamis and I. We really did love each other.

Doctor: So I understand, your majesty, so I have heard.

Lady Macbeth: (*sweetly*) We would walk the castle walls together. We had plans! We had plans for the future. We were both ambitious. Then came the Civil War.

Doctor: (*buttoning his coat*) Ah yes, the Civil War. The invasion from the North. Sweno's attempt to annex Scotland!

Lady Macbeth: My… my husband was so brave. He and Banquo fought the rebels and fought Sweno's army. All would have been well if…

Doctor: (*interrupting*) If he hadn't met the witches, those evil spirits, those supernatural beings. If he had not consorted with evil!

Lady Macbeth: (*thinking*) Just seeing the witches would not have harmed Macbeth. The problem was we both believed their prophecies.

Her voice changes, her body contorts.

All hail Macbeth, hail to thee, Thane of Cawdor! All hail Macbeth, that shalt be king hereafter!

Lady Macbeth laughs a hideous, grotesque laugh.

Doctor: Yes, yes. And the Thane of Cawdor, the first Thane of Cawdor, was linked with the rebels.

Lady Macbeth: My poor husband wrote me a letter telling me all that had happened. By the time I had read the letter, I had made up my mind that old, trusting Duncan, King Duncan, would die!

Doctor:	(*afraid*) Do not tell me anymore. I have heard too much already. I can stay no longer!
	He picks up his black doctor's bag.
Lady Macbeth:	When my husband, Macbeth, returned home, I nagged him to kill the king. I told him he was a coward if he failed to murder Duncan. I told him he didn't love me if he didn't kill the king.
Doctor:	(*stepping backwards, towards the door*) I shall not report what you are saying, your majesty. My lips are sealed.
Lady Macbeth:	(*dancing crazily around the room*) The night of the murder, I took charge. I forced Macbeth to go through with the dreadful deed. I drugged the guards, I took the knives back into Duncan's chamber and smeared the guards with the royal, red blood of King Duncan. For what?
Doctor:	Nobody gains by the doing of evil deeds, your majesty.
Lady Macbeth:	(*fiercely*) I asked evil to enter me. The spirits from blackest hell entered my little body. They tormented me then, as they do now. Night and day, day and night. I thought Macbeth and I would be happy (*crying*) once we had gained the prize. But my husband – he murdered the guards and later murdered his best friend, Banquo. He had the Thane of Fife's wife and children butchered, without my knowledge – (*assumes a mocking voice*) The Thane of Fife had a wife, where is she now?
Doctor:	Madam, goodnight! (*the doctor hurries away muttering to himself*) I must be away from this place, profit again should hardly draw me near.
Lady Macbeth:	(*to herself*) Is there anyone brave enough to listen to my woes?

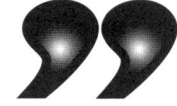

Lesson Notes

Seated

In pairs   Discuss a design for the costume of Lady Macbeth and the set for this scene.

Active

In pairs   Sit down and read the text aloud.
Stand up. When Lady Macbeth speaks her lines, the person playing this role should pursue the doctor around the space (change direction frequently so that you don't end up going round in circles). It should appear as though Lady Macbeth's words are chasing the doctor. He backs away, twists and turns, but cannot escape. When the doctor speaks, both performers freeze where they are.
Discuss the effect of performing the text in this very exaggerated way.

Written

Write the doctor's medical report into Lady Macbeth's physical and mental state, as expressed during this scene.

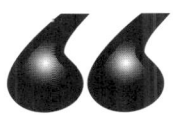

Jenny Meets Clive

A young woman is standing on a platform at a railway station.
She appears agitated.

A young man approaches her.

Clive:	Can I help you? (*embarrassed*) You appear, erm… somewhat distressed.
Jenny:	(*breathless*) I've lost my purse. I think… I think I left it on the train, which is now racing towards Leeds. (*close to tears*). I can't get another train without my purse and I need to get to Peterborough.
Clive:	Well, (*pause*) I could lend you some money. I'm going to Peterborough myself.
Jenny:	(*wiping her eyes*) My mum's been taken ill, seriously ill. She's in hospital. I have to get home quickly. I'm Jenny Pickering, by the way.
Clive:	Clive Thurgood.

They smile awkwardly.

Jenny:	Do you live in Peterborough, Clive?
Clive:	No, no. I'm a travelling salesman.

The train pulls into the station.

Come on! Forget your ticket. Let me help you with your case. Wow, it's heavy.

Jenny:	But, what if an inspector boards the train?
Clive:	(*laughs*) Just tell him you rushed on the train here, at this station. Look, a free carriage! All aboard.

Inside the train.

Jenny:	Must be exciting being a travelling salesman.
Clive:	Yes, yes. You meet all sorts of interesting people, really you do, if you put yourself out.
Jenny:	(*curious*) You always travel by train?
Clive:	Oh yes, always.
Jenny:	(*inquisitive*) But I thought that travelling salesmen had company cars, lovely new cars to speed up and down the motorway. I've never met a train-going travelling salesman.
Clive:	(*falters*) Well, er, I'm the first one you've met then. Perhaps my company is unique.
Jenny:	(*forceful*) What is your company, Clive? Who do you work for? What do you sell? I don't mean to be nosy, I'm just interested.
Clive:	(*hesitant*) Ah, I work for, er, Vacuum Plus. I sell vacuum cleaners.
Jenny:	(*laughing*) Where are the vacuum cleaners, Clive? Not in that black case you're carrying, surely?

Clive:	No, no! The case is full of parts. Vacuum cleaners need all sorts of parts. Fan belts, drives, suction pads – you name it (*he taps on his case*) I have it!
Jenny:	(*intrigued*) I've always wanted to see a suitcase full of vacuum cleaner parts. (*enthusiastic*) Oh, do open up your case. What fun!
Clive:	(*annoyed*) Whoever wants to see vacuum cleaner parts? I can't open it. (*long pause*) I won't! There are some very small parts inside my case. You know, cogs, wheels, screws, nuts and bolts, that sort of thing. (*sharp*) Sorry, can't oblige.
Jenny:	(*shrugs*) Oh, what a shame. Never mind.
	Silence. Jenny fiddles in her bag for a book and starts to read. It is a detective novel.
Clive:	Wouldn't you like to know where I travel? I cover Glasgow, Penrith, Wakefield, Doncaster and Ely.
Jenny:	(*places book on the seat beside her*) Funny you should mention those places. Very odd. A girl has been murdered on a train in each of those places.
Clive:	(*smiles*) Precisely.
Jenny:	(*takes gun from her bag*) Pity you didn't ask me what I did for a living, Clive Thurgood. I work for the police. Inspector Pickering at your service!

Lesson Notes

Seated

In pairs

Allocate who is 'A' and who is 'B'.

- Improvisation 1. 'A' is Jenny. 'B' is a fellow police officer. First, reread the script together. Discuss exactly how Jenny manipulates the situation to catch Clive out. Then, 'A', as Jenny, tells 'B', her colleague, how she went about tracking, tracing and trapping Clive Thurgood. 'B' should ask appropriate questions.
- Improvisation 2. 'A' is a prison officer. 'B' is Clive. It is two months after the trial. 'A' asks 'B' how he was caught. 'B', as Clive, tells the story of his capture. However, he doesn't tell it as it happened. Instead, he exaggerates wildly. End the improvisation with an anticlimax where A, as prison officer, reveals that he knows Inspector Jenny Pickering and therefore has already heard the real version of events.

Active

In pairs

- Rehearse the script two or three times with appropriate actions. Then, put down the scripts and mime the whole scene with no speech. Do this once, then go back to the scripts and pick out the key moments which you think most clearly tell what is happening when you only mime.
- Mime these moments one by one, concentrating on facial expression, reaction, hand gestures and posture.
- Discuss after each key moment whether you think the action is clear enough.
- Now perform the whole scene in mime once more. Is it clearer than your first go?

Written

As a newspaper reporter, write an article featuring an interview with Inspector Pickering detailing the investigation that led to the capture of Clive Thurgood.

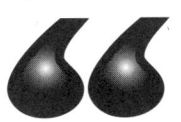

Aliens View Earth

Two aliens are hovering above Earth on a space ship. They are wondering whether it is worth invading the planet Earth.

Alien 1: (*breathes deeply*) A wonderful planet. A varied climate. Full of fresh air and mountains and rivers, and a wealth of fascinating wildlife. Indeed, a planet ripe for invasion.

Alien 2: (*scans a computer*) Hold on a moment, sir. Your enthusiasm may be misplaced. Just take a look at what the computer is showing us.

Alien 1: Great god Mixitus in the sky! This can't be true, can it? Ozone layer depleted, global warming, overpopulation of the planet... What's caused all this?

Alien 2: The computer blames a species known as *Homo Sapiens*, although they call themselves humans. This primitive life form is destroying all the other life forms and is likely to destroy itself.

Alien 1: Carcadoo, my friend, let's beam down and see what the planet is really like.

Alien 2: Are you sure that's wise, sir? It could be dangerous.

Alien 1: Have courage, Carcadoo. I'm curious to see for myself.

The aliens beam down to planet Earth, landing in a busy city. Cars zoom past them in all directions.

Alien 2: So, their transport is built out of a ton of heavy metal, and all those brick boxes are hardly designed to save energy. (*points to people entering a fast-food restaurant*) And just look at how humans worship!

Alien 1: Yes, strange religion. They enter the bright temple, sit in plastic seats and eat great slabs of purified meat wedged inside slabs of bread.

Alien 2: Yet they seem to derive pleasure from it. Very peculiar.

A thick fog descends.

Alien 1: Carcadoo, what is happening? What is this thick yellow blanket rolling towards us? Is it a secret weapon of the human race?

Alien 2: No, no, sir. It is called smog. The computer warned me about this. Apparently humans create smog by driving too many of their primitive vehicles. The smog causes accidents and even death to some of these people.

Alien 1: How strange! Perhaps their leaders want some of the humans culled to stop the overpopulation (*they hear noises*). And those humans making all that noise. Is this a ritual chant?

Alien 2: No, no, sir. Those humans falling out of the Bacchus Temple – which they call a pub – have drunk too much and they get very loud. Sometimes they hurt themselves or others. This is called having a good time. (*pause*) The two shouting at each other are man and wife.

Alien 1:	Ah, so these people don't marry for love
Alien 2:	Well they do, sir, but it seems their feelings can change.
Alien 1:	Humans are strange creatures. They appear to have no constancy, no loyalty to one another.
Alien 2:	(*nods*) These creatures do seem to be selfish in so many ways.
Alien 1:	(*decisive*) I think, Carcadoo, we will avoid this planet. We'll beam back up to the spaceship and take a look at planet Alcher XI – a place similar to Earth, but devoid of humans.
Alien 2:	Good idea, sir. Humans are a strange unintelligent life form! Let's leave them to destroy their own planet.
	They zoom off.

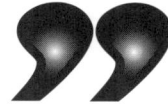

Lesson Notes

Seated

In groups

- Discuss whether you think the aliens' assessment of the situation on Earth is either fair or accurate. Say why.
- Consider other aspects of life on Earth which other life forms may find disturbing. Say why. In your groups, record these aspects under main headings. (e.g. war, poverty, conflict, famine, overuse of pesticides, smoking etc.) Elect a spokesperson to comment on certain aspects of life on Earth. What is it about an alien viewpoint that makes us view human behaviour in a different way?

Active

In groups

In groups of 3 or 4. Improvise the following:

- Two people in the group are to play the two aliens who observed Earth. The other person (or pair) should be a third (and fourth) alien who asks whether Earth proved a suitable site for invasion. Aliens 1 and 2 must describe all the reasons why they wouldn't recommend going anywhere near Earth. Alien 3 (and 4) should ask questions to prompt more descriptions of humans. Alien 3 (and 4) is amazed to hear the grim details and this amazement should increase to complete shock. Aliens 1 and 2 can use ideas generated during the previous discussion to add details of awful human behaviour.

Written

- In role as an alien who has observed Earth and human behaviour, write a letter addressed to all humankind listing six of the worst aspects of human behaviour that you saw. Your aim is to persuade humans to change their attitude. After describing each of the six aspects, present strong reasons why humans should change their behaviour.

Adaptation

Adaptations are usually from pre-twentieth century stories. This is from a Sherlock Holmes short story by Arthur Conan Doyle, entitled *A Case of Identity*.

A Case of Identity

Sherlock Holmes and Doctor Watson are sitting either side of the fireplace in Holmes' lodgings at Baker Street. A coal fire is burning brightly.

Holmes: Life is stranger than anything that the mind of man can invent.

Dr Watson: (*thinking*) I am not convinced of it. The cases that come to light in the paper are vulgar enough. You help people who are puzzled and so life offers interest and variety to you.

Holmes: (*shakes his head*) There is nothing so unnatural as the commonplace.

Dr Watson: (*picking up the morning paper*) Let's see who is right. We'll put our separate theories to a practical test. Here is the first heading I come across (*reads*) 'A husband's cruelty to his wife'. The usual stuff – the other woman, the drink, the push, the blow, the bruise – it happens all the time. Even the crudest writer could do better than that!

Holmes: (*reflects*) Ah, the Dundas separation case. I know a bit about that one. The husband is teetotal. There was no other woman involved. (*brightens*) The wife wants a separation because Dundas winds up every meal by taking out his false teeth and hurling them at his wife. What storyteller would think of such a plot? So Watson, I am right, you are wrong!

There is a sudden knock on the door.

Bell Boy: A Miss Mary Sutherland to see you, sir.

Mary Sutherland enters. A small figure, dressed in black, she is a spinster who is plain and fussy-looking.

Holmes: (*to Mary*) Do sit down.

Mary Sutherland sits in the spare armchair, away from the fire.

Do you not find that with your short sight, it is a little trying to do much typewriting?

Mary: I did at first, but now I know where the letters are without looking (*she is suddenly aware of what Holmes has said*). But... how did you know that, Mr Holmes?

Holmes: (*grinning*) I have trained myself to see things that others overlook.

	Otherwise, why consult me?
Mary:	(*quietly*) I came to see you, sir, because I want to know what has become of Mr Hosmer Angel.
Holmes:	But why come here in such a hurry?
Mary:	(*shocked*) How did you know that? But it is true. Mr Windebank, my stepfather, would do nothing to help me find Mr Hosmer Angel. He refused to see the police, or to see you. (*pause*) I argued with him and left quickly. When my father died, mother married Mr Windebank in haste.
Holmes:	I see. And how did you meet Mr Hosmer Angel?
Mary:	(*blushing*) I met Mr Angel at the gas fitter's ball. I went with my mother and we met some of my dead father's old friends. My stepfather was not pleased when he found out! He'd gone on a business trip to France at the time.
Holmes:	(*walking around the room*) Asking a personal question, are you well-off, Miss Sutherland?
Mary:	I have some money from the sale of my father's business, but my Uncle Ned in Auckland, New Zealand, left me a huge sum of money. I only touch the interest and I give that to my parents. I do not need money, not until I marry, which I never will if you can't find Mr Hosmer Angel.
Holmes:	(*faces her*) And tell me, when did you last see Mr Angel?
Mary:	(*weeping*) The day before our wedding.
Dr Watson:	(*interrupting*) Wedding? Oh, I say.
Mary:	Mr Angel proposed to me the day after the ball. I met him in the park and we went for a walk.
	Mary sobs.
Dr Watson:	(*soothing*) There, there, Miss Sutherland.
Holmes:	What do you know about Mr Hosmer Angel, Mary? What does he look like? Where does he work?
Mary:	(*smiling*) He was such a gentle man. He was very shy. He would rather walk with me in the evening than in the daylight. Even his voice was gentle. He'd had glandular fever as a boy and it had left him with a weak voice. He usually whispered. His eyes were weak, like mine, and he wore tinted glasses against the glare. Oh, and he had a great black moustache!
Holmes:	(*thinking*) So, when Mr Angel met your stepfather, what happened?
Mary:	They never met. Mr Angel asked me to marry him. I told mother and my stepfather argued his reluctance.
Holmes:	(*walking around the room again*) Ah, I see. (*pause*) Try to let Mr Hosmer Angel vanish from your memory as he has done from your eyes.
Mary:	(*tearful*) Then… I shan't see him again?

Holmes:	(*looking out of the window*) I fear not, Miss Sutherland. I fear not.
Dr Watson:	(*kindly*) I shall see you to your carriage, Miss Sutherland.
	Dr Watson and Mary Sutherland leave. She is sobbing. Holmes sits on a chair, his hands clasped together, as if in prayer. Watson returns.
Dr Watson:	I say, Holmes, how did you know Miss Sutherland was a short-sighted typist?
Holmes:	The woman's sleeve tells us all. The double line a little above the wrist, where the typewriter presses against the table, was beautifully defined. I glanced at her face and observed the mark of a pince-nez at either side of her nose.
Dr Watson:	But… but how did you know she was in such a hurry?
Holmes:	(*stands, hands clasped behind his back*) The woman dressed well, but wore odd boots and the laces were undone. Why would a careful dresser take such little care about her feet unless she was in a hurry?
Dr Watson:	(*sadly*) Well, it's a pity Holmes, that you can't solve the mystery as quickly.
Holmes:	(*turns to face Dr Watson*) But I have! The mystery is solved!
Watson:	(*shocked*) Who was Mr Angel and why did he desert Miss Sutherland? He has no motive, no gain!
Holmes:	The only person who gains is the wicked stepfather, Mr Windebank. He and his wife thought of a cruel trick to keep the money sent from New Zealand. That money would disappear if Miss Sutherland married.
Dr Watson:	(*confused*) Explain, Holmes.
Holmes:	(*quickly*) Mr Windebank claimed a business trip to France, but he stayed in London and disguised himself as Hosmer Angel, to fool his stepdaughter. He knew that if she fell in love and Mr Angel disappeared, she'd wait for him for at least ten years – she's the faithful sort.
Dr Watson:	(*shocked*) That is cruel. What will you do to expose this villain?
Holmes:	Windebank has not broken the law. What should I do? If I tell Mary Sutherland, she will never believe me. Remember the old Persian saying? There is danger for him who taketh the tiger cub, and danger also for him who snatches a delusion from a woman! So you see, Watson, life is stranger than anything that the mind of man could invent.
Dr Watson:	Well Holmes, what will you do?
Holmes:	(*turning to face the audience*) What do you think I should do?

Lesson Notes

Seated

Class discussion

- Answer the question. What do you think Holmes should do? Give reasons for your opinion.
- Which parts of the plot are believable? Which parts are unbelievable? Why?

In pairs

- One person plays the role of a journalist and the other plays Mary. The journalist interviews Mary.

Active

Improvise a scene where:

- Mary returns home to her mother and Mr Windebank. She is extremely upset and tells them what Sherlock Holmes has said to her. They (falsely and unconvincingly) try to comfort her, but they are obviously pleased at her protestations that she will never marry anyone else.
- Sherlock Holmes arrives and tells Mary that he has found Mr Angel. How does the stepfather react? Build dramatic tension towards a climax. How does it end? Does Sherlock Holmes reveal what the stepfather has done or does he let the stepfather inadvertently reveal what he has done?

Written

Write a newspaper article reporting the deception and Mary's reaction when she discovered the truth. Or, write Mary's letter to Sherlock Holmes after Mary has discovered the truth.

Spoof

Spoofs poke fun at, or imitate, well-known stories in a humorous way. You will recognise this story. It is taken from Charles Dickens' story, *Oliver Twist*.

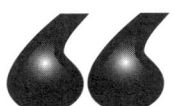 ## Oliver Twit

The Mortgrave Children's Home, North London. Mr Grumble, the warden, is in a really bad mood. He is clutching a radio in his right hand. The children are sitting on a bench, waiting for their food.

Martin:	Hey, watch out, Old Grumble is about. He looks as if he's in one of his moods.
Anna:	Yeah, Arsenal lost again!
Oliver:	(*shouts*) Mr Grumble, did Arsenal lose at home?
	Martin and Anna bury their faces in their hands.
Mr Grumble:	I'm the warden. That means I'm in charge of you, young Twit! Now, I don't want you making any trouble. I don't want you winding me up, understood?
Oliver:	Yes, sir… only, I just wanted to say I'm sorry that Arsenal lost at home to relegation-threatened Sunderland, sir.
Martin:	Look at those beefburgers, are they supposed to be our lunch?
Anna:	(*to Martin*) Vomit burgers more like! The last time I ate one, I was ill all night.
Martin:	They're too small for me. A mouse could have eaten mine.
Anna:	It probably did, that's how I got food poisoning when I nicked half of yours!
Martin:	Perhaps we should ask for double cheeseburgers.
Oliver:	Oh no, I don't think we should do that.
Martin:	Why? Why shouldn't we ask for more?
Oliver:	Well… er… it would make trouble, wouldn't it? Grumble wouldn't like us asking for more.
Anna:	He couldn't do anything about it – not if we all stood together. We could form a united front.
Oliver:	Yes, but somebody has to actually ask for more.

Anna:	True.
Oliver:	Who's going to be stupid enough to ask for more?
Martin:	Let's draw lots. Whoever has the smallest straw has to ask Grumble for more.
	Anna finds three straws from old plastic orange cups. She breaks one and offers it to Oliver.
Oliver:	(*pleased*) Oh, I say. Me first, thanks.
	He takes the straw offered, which is the smallest.
	Now, what did you give me this straw for? I've just had a drink.
Anna:	You have to ask Mr Grumble for a double cheeseburger.
Oliver:	(*confused*) Why me?
Tina/Martin:	'Cause you've picked the shortest straw, that's why!
Oliver:	Yes, but… (*he sees Martin has clenched his fists*) Oh, all right!
	Oliver creeps up to Mr Grumble. He coughs.
	Mr Grumble, sir!
Grumble:	(*bad-tempered*) Yes, boy, what do you want now?
Oliver:	(*afraid*) The, er… vomit burgers are too small and… er…
Grumble:	(*angry*) The what burgers?
Oliver:	(*worried*) That's what we call them, sir, vom…
Grumble:	(*interrupting*) Never mind. Just get on with what you want to say.
Oliver:	(*timidly*) We were wondering, sir, if we could have double cheeseburgers for lunch, sir?
Grumble:	(*even more angry*) Double cheeseburgers? Are you out of your tiny little mind, Twit, or what? Double cheeseburgers? You ungrateful boy! This is the last straw!
Oliver:	(*thinking he could help*) Short straw, sir. I picked the short straw. Martin picked the last straw.
Grumble:	(*confused*) What?
Oliver:	I'd like some cheese straws.
Anna:	(*to Grumble*) Get rid of 'im, sir, 'e's doin' my 'ead in!
Grumble:	(*an idea occurs to him*) Yes, good one, Anna. Mr Sowerkrout needs an apprentice. Get Mr Sowerkrout at once!
	Enter Mr Sowerkrout. He is dressed in black and has a mournful expression on his face.
Grumble:	I have an apprentice for you, Sowerkrout. A good, quiet boy.
Sowerkrout:	(*to Oliver*) Come with me. What's your name, boy?
Grumble:	(*for Oliver*) Twit, sir.

Sowerkrout:	(briskly) Yes, yes. I know you are, Grumble. You always have been. I want to know the boy's name.
Grumble:	He's called Twit, sir – Oliver Twit!
Sowerkrout:	Well, come along, Twit.
	Oliver follows Mr Sowerkrout.
	(to Oliver) I'm an undertaker, Twit. I deal in bodies – dead ones. I like a harsh winter and a sickly spring. The more deaths, the more money I make.
Oliver:	What about a good road accident, a multiple pile-up?
Sowerkrout:	(surprised) Excellent! You're a natural, Twit. A nice foggy day and a multiple pile-up on the M25 and the phone never stops ringing.
	They arrive outside a large, gloomy house.
Sowerkrout:	Here we are, Twit… here we are. Sowerkrout the undertaker. This is my place. You'll sleep with the coffins.
	A large, ugly, spotty-faced youth appears.
Noah:	Morning, Mr Sowerkrout.
Sowerkrout:	(glances at watch) Afternoon Noah. Slept through the morning, have we?
Noah:	No, sir, the pipes burst. Almost caused a flood, sir.
Sowerkrout:	(uses his humour) Ah, well, don't build an ark, Noah. Now take young Twit to inspect the coffins.
Noah:	(watching Oliver walk the wrong way) This way, Twit!
	Noah shows Oliver a row of coffins.
	Ever seen a stiff, Twit?
Oliver:	A stiff?
Noah:	Dead body.
Oliver:	No. (scared) No, I haven't.
Noah:	(matter of fact) About time you did see a stiff, Oliver old pal. Young girl, died this morning – nasty accident, Oliver. Lift up the coffin lid and take a look at your first dead body.
Oliver:	(shrinks back) N-no, I couldn't.
Noah:	Ollie, old mate, you must. Mr Sowerkrout will be asking you to lift dead bodies into coffins. I do it all the time, second nature to me!
Oliver:	(hesitates) No, I…
Noah:	(coaxing) Don't be shy, you seen one dead body, you seen the lot! (forceful) Go on!
	Oliver approaches the coffin and gingerly lifts the lid. A girl suddenly sits bolt upright. Oliver screams and runs away. The girl and Noah laugh.
Oliver:	(frightened) Oh, oh.

Noah:	(*laughing*) What a picture you looked, Twit! Ha, ha. Caught you there. Let me introduce you to Charlotte, Mr Sowerkrout's maid.
Charlotte:	(*climbing out of coffin*) Hi, Ollie babe!
	Oliver runs away from them both and out of the house. He sees a signpost marked Central London and he walks on.
Artful:	(*runs up to Oliver*) You run away, 'ave you?
Oliver:	Yes, afraid so.
Artful:	You've just met the right bloke, you 'ave. I'll take you to Fag-in-mouth – that's not 'is real name, but he'll kill hisself one of these days. Tell yer what, he'll get us a couple of tickets for the Chelsea v Arsenal match, if we treat him kind.
	Artful takes Oliver to Fag-in.
Fag-in:	(*coughs a smoker's cough*) Ah, a new boy.
Artful:	Calls 'imself, er…
Oliver:	Twit. Oliver Twit.
Fag-in:	Well, young Twit, just watch me. I walk around with me wallet out of me pocket, see? Now watch Artful nick me wallet, with me club card and me credit cards and the tickets for the Chelsea v Arsenal match in!
Oliver:	(*horrified*) But, but that's stealing.
Fag-in:	(*patient*) Technically speaking, yes, you're right Oliver, I'll grant you that! Artful steals, nicks, pinches, swipes me wallet. But you knows he's goin' to do it, so it ain't stealin', it's a game.
	Enter Zoe, a bouncy, friendly type. She takes one look at Oliver and knows he's not a thief.
Zoe:	Oh, ain't he cute! (*points at Oliver*) Fag-in, you brute, don't corrupt the little fella.
Fag-in:	(*acting innocent*) Corrupt him? Who me? Would I do a thing like that? Come here little Twit, would I do a thing like that?
Oliver:	(*to Zoe*) No, Mr Fag-in's a kind old man. We're just playing games.
Zoe:	(*laughs*) Don't give me that, Fag-in. I'll tell Mr Luke Brownlow. Don't you worry, he'll get the low-down from me. You'll be in clink for years, and they'll throw away the key. You'll rot in jail, Fag-in.
	Enter Short-Sight, a desperate, overweight bully
Short-Sight:	Just shot me dog and ate it, Fag-in. I was that hungry.
Fag-in:	(*upset*) You've made a right pig's ear of things, Short-Sight.
Short-Sight:	More of a dog's dinner, really.
Zoe:	Eaten a dog! I'm not standin' for that. I'm fetchin' the police.
	She blows on a tin whistle. Mr Brownlow appears, with a gun and a belt full of hand grenades.
Fag-in:	(*afraid*) Brownlow!

Short-Sight:	You'll not catch me alive.
	He mistakes the window for a door and falls to his death.
	Aaaah!
Oliver:	(*matter-of-fact*) Sowerkrout will like this!
Brownlow:	The police are arriving, you're all under arrest.
Oliver:	(*steps forward*) I'm innocent. I'm here because all I did was ask Mr Grumble for a double cheeseburger.
Fag-in:	(*shocked*) A double cheeseburger? Did you say a double cheeseburger, young Twit?
Zoe:	(*licks her lips*) Yum.
Brownlow:	That's what I like, a boy with spirit. Oliver, you will live in my mansion and eat as many cheeseburgers as you like. From now on, you will be my son, Oliver Brownlow!
Oliver:	(*to audience*) So who were the real twits? Me, or Anna and Martin? I've got a cushy number and they're still with old Grumble at the children's home. Don't be impressed by names and appearances, eh?

Lesson Notes

Seated

In groups

Spoofs are intended to take a well-known story and to imitate or poke fun at it in a humorous way. When writing a spoof, the author will start with the most well-known and recognisable elements of the plot and characters, and will then devise ways of twisting, changing or updating those elements. For example, in this script, the scriptwriter, Keith West, has changed the main character's surname from Oliver Twist to Oliver Twit. He has taken the main points of the original story: Oliver, an orphan in a workhouse, asks for more food. He is apprenticed, runs away, falls in with Fagin and his group of child-thieves and is eventually reunited with his family. Keith West has updated these elements into a 21st-century setting and changed the names and situations and adapted them to add humour. A spoof is intended to seem ridiculous.

First, in your groups, allocate parts and read through the script. Discuss the changes the writer has made to the original story. Then, still in your groups, take a well-known fairy tale and discuss how you could replay it as a spoof. Fold a piece of A4 paper in half, on one side list the main elements of your chosen tale. Use these details to discuss and make notes on how you would change and update the tale for humorous effect. For example, Cinderella has been subject to many changes and radical rewritings. You could try your own 'Cinder-fella', where Cinders is a boy or perhaps 'Cyber-fella', which would be a futuristic or robotic version. Report back to the rest of the class on the main details of your spoof plot.

Active

Act out the opening of the fairytale spoof you have planned (as above). Do not tell your audience which tale you are spoofing. They should be able to tell immediately by the characters and the recognisable, but changed, elements of the plot.

Written

Use the details discussed in your group to write the full version of a spoof fairy tale.

Absurd

An absurd play is neither rational nor logical. Absurd plays may take place in a world similar to our own, but a world without logic or reason.

 Meeting Cutter

Two people are sitting in a café. They are possibly mother and son.

Characters
Ida – an old lady
Tony – middle-aged man – possibly her son
Tex – a brash, big man, about Tony's age.
Café manager

Ida:	(*to Tony*) You know, my teeth don't fit. The dentist (*slurps her tea*) didn't do a good job and now my teeth are all out of line.
Tony:	(*between mouthfuls of bacon sandwich*) Oh!
Ida:	That means I can't chew properly. (*confidentially*) Gives me wind!
Tony:	(*grimaces*) I think Cutter will be along soon.
Ida:	Why do you call that man Cutter?
Tony:	(*sulky*) Don't know – always have. We all call him Cutter. He's into roses (*thinks*) or was, at least.
Ida:	(*spilling tea down her chin*) Into roses? I wish the youth of today would talk proper. What do you mean, into roses?
Tony:	I mean, he grows roses and he has an interest in roses.
Ida:	(*picking up her bacon sandwich*) Glad we came in here. I couldn't have walked another yard. It's my shoes, they pinch and…
	A big, broad-shouldered man sits at their table.
Tex:	(*loud*) Good to see you, Cutter!
Tony:	Sorry, you're mistaken. We're waiting for Cu…
Tex:	(*slaps Tony on the back, so that he spills his tea*) Don't give me that, Cutter, mate!
Ida:	…the chiropodist didn't do my feet properly this time. She made a mess of the toenail.
Tony:	(*to Tex*) I've never seen you before in my life.
Tex:	(*punches Tony on his arm, so that he spills his tea*) Oh, you are a card! We came here together, years ago (*thinks*) or was it months ago?
Tony:	(*slowly*) Cutter is the person who grows roses. He's a different build to me. Stocky fella. He's my mate (*thinks*) or was!
Tex:	(*laughs*) Growing roses? Not here, not with all that mildew about. Fog chokes roses and the fog's thick around here.

Tony:	(helpful) Maybe he grows the roses somewhere else?
Tex:	(looks at Tony with amusement) Somewhere else? There ain't anywhere else!
Ida:	(rubs her foot) Do you think I should have the bunion seen to?
Tex:	(to Tony) Don't you recognise your old mate, Cutter?
Tony:	(defiant) Never seen you in my life, before now.
Ida:	Well that's odd (confused) I've lost my glasses case. Have you seen my case, Tony?
Tony:	(thinks) You must have left it in the clothes shop.
Ida:	(irritable) I can't go back there, not with my feet.
Tex:	(laughs) Whose feet will you walk back with then, old lady?
Tony:	(cross) Look you… I… I… I don't like the drift of your conversation. I don't like the tone of your voice. In fact, I don't like anything about you.
Tex:	(menacing) You don't? Don't I suit then, Cutter, mate? Bit of a snob now, are you?
Tony:	(shouts hysterically) I'm not Cutter!
Tex:	Yeah, yeah. So you say, so you say.
Ida:	Ouch, I think I've got indigestion. What I need is peace and quiet. I don't like loud noises.
Tex:	(brandishes a gun) No one messes around with old Tex.
	He shoots Tony, who dies very theatrically and slumps across the table.
Ida:	(to Tex) I told you, young man, I don't like loud noises. You'll set my ears buzzing for days.
	Café Manager walks up to the table with a tea towel slung across his shoulder.
Café Manager:	(indicating Tony) Is he asleep?
Ida:	Sleep? Did someone mention sleep? I never sleep these days. I lie awake for hours on end. But there's no dawn here. This is a place without hope, without salt and light.
Café Manager:	(to Tex, but indicating Tony) Is he asleep?
Tex:	(loud and brash) Not asleep, he's dead.
Café Manager:	(sadly) Aren't we all?
Tex:	(quieter) Yes, but he's dead, dead. (proud) I just shot him.
Café Manager:	(looking hard at Tex) Hey, I know you. You're Cutter. You're the one who used to grow those scented roses – a long time ago. When I was young. I used to smell your roses, after a light rain. They were like glimpses of something. Something better.
Tex:	(indicates Tony) I'm not Cutter, he was!

Café Manager: (*dreamily*) Everything smells the same here, like rancid butter. Taste – I can taste nothing, nothing that isn't putrid, spoiled.

Ida: (*tearful*) How will I manage without Tony? (*to Tex*) You shouldn't have shot him, he was useful to me. Whatever shall I do? This is a harsh world.

Café Manager: (*thoughtful*) What did Abraham Lincoln say? Something about people being about as happy as they want to be?

Ida: Yes, well, I'm happy… or would be if I were younger, more alive.

Café Manager: (*to Tex*) Come on Cutter, you might as well plant more roses. We're here for a long time after all.

Tex: (*defiant*) I'm not Cutter, mate. He was a tall, thin man, not like me at all. And you can't grow roses here, the mildew.

Café Manager: (*sadly*) And the fog, it'll choke them.

Lesson Notes

Seated

Class discussion

Absurd drama is sometimes used as a way of commenting on the nature of human existence. In other words, we, the audience, are presented with something so bizarre, improbable, unlikely or unreal that it encourages us to ask bigger questions. In this piece, some questions to consider are:

- Where do you think the action really takes place? Some people have thought that it is set in hell. Others have considered that it suggests that hell exists only as a state of mind. What do you think? In the discussion, support your point of view (there is no 'right' answer) by picking out particular lines and explain what impression they give you.
- Who is Cutter? What do you think? Is he one person – Tony or Tex, or someone else? Or is he a group of people? Or does he represent a point of view?
- Look at everything that Ida says. What do we learn about her character? Does she remind you of anyone you have ever known or seen on television? Do you think that the author is using this character to make a point? If so, what point is being made?

Active

In groups

Take the section of text from the line *Ida: Do you think I should have the bunion seen to?* to *Tony: I'm not Cutter!*

Act out this section so that you can repeat it perfectly each time – with exactly the same movements and vocal intonation. Now perform it as a piece of looped dialogue (when you get to the end of the section, begin again, without pause, until you have performed it through three times). Comment on what effect this creates.

Now try a speeded-up version, followed by a slowed-down one with a final rewind version (as though you are a video being played that is going wrong.) Again, comment on the effect.

Written

Imagine you are the café manager. Note the important events of the scene in bullet-point form as follows:

- Ida and Tony in café
- Ida complaining
- Tex enters

Melodrama

Melodrama exaggerates the probable. It takes the 'suspension of disbelief' to the limits. Melodrama originally meant 'drama with music'. Nowadays melodrama relies on extravagant action and emotion, with strong visual and sound effects. Many early horror films were melodramatic.

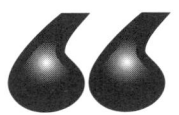 ## Kelloway and the Dark Arts

Characters
Kevin Kelloway – a man willing to do anything to win back his loved one
Mr Rusling – an old man, dressed as a wizard
Judy Mills (née Lacombe) – Kevin's loved one
Melissa – a beautiful woman
Young man – sent to warn Kevin
Don – an earnest young man, in love
Waitress – sent to warn Kevin
Devil 1
Devil 2

Kevin:	(*full of self-pity*) I want her back, the girl I have always loved! Judy Lacombe, the woman my father forbade me to marry.
Rusling:	(*grave*) Ah, as I have already told you, Kevin Kelloway, you can gain the powers that will bring her back to you – gain the dark powers, practise the dark arts and all will be yours.
	Thunder outside.
Kevin:	(*confident*) I have practised, all these years, and I am ready.
Rusling:	(*coughs sadly*) I am an old man, ready for the grave. I can no longer conjure spirits, but you, you have time on your hands.
	Lightning flashes.
	Now! Conjure her now, Kevin Kelloway (*proud*), new Prince of the Dark Arts.
	Kevin raises his arms upwards, as if in prayer. There is a crashing sound and a middle-aged woman stands before Kevin.

Kevin:	(*shocked*) Who are you?
Judy:	(*speaks quietly*) I am Judy Mills, once known as Judy Lacombe, long since married.
Kevin:	But… but you cannot be the Judy I adored in my early years, the one I have loved and not seen for thirty years. There is grey in your hair, your body is not slim and lithe, as I remember!
Judy:	(*patiently*) Oh Kevin, what did you expect? *Your* hair is grey, *your* face is lined. You didn't think I would remain unattached all these years, did you? I haven't been summoned from Shangri-La, you know. I've lived a tough life in Basildon.
Kevin:	(*hides his face*) Go. Get away from me. I'd rather keep my dreams until my dying day than see this mocking reality.

Judy vanishes.

Is that why I studied the dark arts? All that hard work for so little return? Why did I work all these years, (*scoffs*) to see an ordinary, harassed, middle-aged woman with all her youth and beauty gone?

Below, in the street, children mock each other. Thin, mocking voices float upwards.

Rusling:	(*laughs*) You cannot stop the march of time, Kevin Kelloway. If you want to see beauty, conjure up the most beautiful woman in all England.
Kevin:	Good idea!

Outside, thunder rolls ominously. Children in the street shout in voices that show both excitement and fear. Kevin Kelloway spreads his arms outwards and chants. Before him is a beautiful woman, dressed in white.

At last! Perfection! And what is your name?

Melissa:	Melissa… but I am unhappy.

She bursts into tears.

My fiancé is leaving tonight to go on a business trip. This is Don's last evening with me and I have booked a table for two at Palermo's Italian restaurant. Why make me so unhappy when I could be with Don?

Rusling:	Why not make her unhappy?
Kevin:	(*thinking of his love for Judy, years ago*) Go!

Melissa vanishes.

Rusling:	(*patient*) Kevin, you do not understand evil! That Melissa girl could become your wife. You could ask the dark demons to destroy the train that Melissa's fiancé is travelling on. He could die tonight.
Kevin:	I have a better plan. Let me conjure the powers of darkness. We shall dine at Palermo's, my old friend. We shall see for ourselves what this Don fellow is like.

The odd couple stand outside the busy Italian restaurant in London. A young man approaches.

Young Man:	(*confidentially*) Kevin Kelloway, it is not too late to repent. Turn away from evil before your heart is hardened and you despise all that is good.
Rusling:	(*averts his eyes from the young man*) I cannot bear the goodness, I cannot.
Young Man:	(*to Kevin*) You are being tricked, you are not really able to conjure up the people you want to see, it is only an illusion to trick you. Evil spirits are deceiving you for their own malevolent purposes.
Rusling:	(*to Kevin*) It is not true, not true. Come inside the restaurant and we shall have fun!
	Rusling drags Kevin inside the restaurant. They sit at a table next to Melissa and her fiancé.
Melissa:	(*to Don*) I shall miss you while you are away.
	They hold hands across the table.
Don:	(*light-hearted*) When I return, we shall marry. I'll find a job in the country somewhere.
Rusling:	(*to Kevin*) Let's have some sport. Conjure the food to move.
	Don's soup hovers in mid-air and tips over Melissa.
Don:	(*upset*) Melissa, my dear, I am so sorry. I'm sure the soup moved!
Melissa:	(*smiling as she wipes the soup from her skirt*) Never mind, my darling, I know you are normally so careful. (*she spots Kevin and Rusling*) Don, you know that daydream I had earlier, about meeting that awful man? He's sitting next to us. Isn't that strange?
Don:	Weird!
Waitress:	(*at Kevin's table, she whispers to him*) You do not need to practise the dark arts, it's not too late! (*aloud*) Have you studied the menu? What would you like, sir?
Rusling:	(*to Kevin*) Don's train leaves early tomorrow morning. You could destroy the thing and claim the beautiful girl for yourself. You have the power to keep her under your spell, like the child in the crystal palace.
Waitress:	(*whispers to Kevin*) And destroy all the other people on the train, too? Could you live with that?
Rusling:	(*adjusting his hearing aid*) What did the waitress just say?
Waitress:	(*to Rusling*) I said the plaice was all you could afford and your old body is turning to fat.
Rusling:	(*annoyed*) Cheek! I might be old, but I'm still good for a trick or two.
	Rusling mumbles to himself.
Waitress:	Sorry, Oscar Rusling, your evil cannot harm me. You cannot touch me with your foolish spells.
	Rusling stands up and shouts incantations at the waitress, who stares at him with her wide blue eyes.

Rusling:	(*knowing he is beaten*) So, you are one of the good ones, eh? I shall try my strongest magic, even though I told Kevin Kelloway I was too old for that. I will prove everyone wrong. I shall prove the devil wrong!
	He shouts incantations and falls down in a fit.
Devil 1:	(*barges past onlookers*) Excuse me, excuse me, won't keep you more than a moment.
Devil 2:	We've come for this evil soul. It belongs with us, in the place of no return. (*to Kevin Kelloway*) We shall be back for you, when your body gives up its soul.

Lesson Notes
Seated

In pairs

Interview Kevin Kelloway for the radio. One person is to be the interviewer and one to be Kevin. Devise your own questions, for example:

- Why did you get involved with Rusling?
- Tell us about the Judy of thirty years ago. What was so special about her that your adoration lasted all your life?
- Why did your father forbid you to marry her?
- What happened next, after Rusling died? What was your reaction?
- What do you intend to do now?

Active
In groups

In a group of 3 (plus a director), take from the beginning of the scene, up to the line *Kevin: At last! Perfection! And what is your name?* Act out this section, concentrating on the exaggeration needed for a melodramatic performance. You need to think about:

- exaggerated posture
- larger than life movements
- very animated facial expressions
- huge, noticeable mannerisms and gestures
- over-reaction to the other performers

A good warm-up exercise prior to this activity is to gauge the level of your exaggeration. Using levels 1-10 of exaggeration as a basis, level 5 would be speaking in a normal voice at normal volume. Level 1 would be whispering in a very timid way. Level 10 would be performing with all the over-reaction, exaggeration, facial expression and whole-body expression you can muster. Take the phrase 'You are evil'. All stand and move around the room. When the teacher instructs, 'Go to level —' (number between 1 and 10), you freeze. All simultaneously say the phrase at the level instructed.

Written

In role as a director, write up notes to accompany the section of script used in the activity above. Describe exactly how the performers should:

- move
- speak
- relate and react to each other
- use non-verbal reaction and interaction
- use their faces
- pace their speech
- set the length of their pauses
- use props

In your notes, use character names to identify which speeches you are talking about.

Farce

The object of farce is to make people laugh. Characters find themselves in embarrassing situations that change very quickly. The possibility of coincidence is pushed to the limit.

The Bigamist

Characters
Oliver Diamond – a bigamist
Helen Diamond – his wife in Cambridge
Pauline Diamond – his wife in Bradford
Derek Mumford – a friend
Mrs Crampsie – Pauline's Mum

Scene One

The Cambridge apartment, early morning.

Oliver: (*packs bag*) I'm off with the lorry, to Bradford again.

Helen: (*disappointed*) Oh Oliver, I'm tired of you sharing half a life with me. I'll come with you to Bradford. Wouldn't that be really something?

Oliver: (*horrified*) Ah, yes. (*thinks*) But you can't!

Helen: Why ever not, sweetie-pie? It's half term, I know a nice little bed and breakfast we could go to. I can take my marking along!

Oliver: (*concerned*) A B&B in Bradford? Where?

Helen: (*picks up a red pen*) Oh Oliver, you do sound stressed. You have been working so hard, driving that big lorry up and down the busy motorways all these months, while all I've done is taught kids, marked books, attended meetings and been inspected. (*pause*) A break would do you good.

Oliver: (*in a whisper*) Which B&B, my dear? (*develops nervous twitch*) Which?

Helen: (*bright*) The Liston House, next to Liston Park in Bradford. (*concerned*) Dear Oliver, you've turned awfully pale.

Oliver: Cancel it at once!

Helen: Cancel? Why sweetie-pie (*laughs*), anyone would think you were keeping something from me.

Oliver: (*quickly*) No, no, not at all. It's just that all the drivers tell me it's a… erm… dirty, dingy little place.

Helen: (*shocked*) But my mum tells me it's very pleasant. It's non-smoking, vegetarian, no teenagers. Oh Oliver, you'll love the place. It sounds like a home from home.

Some time later, the Diamonds arrive outside The Liston House, Bradford.

Oliver: (*hesitates*) Ah, I'll just get the cases and, er, book us in, Helen. You go on ahead.

Helen:	But…
	Oliver dashes off.
Mrs Crampsie:	(*opens door*) Hello, you must be Mrs Diamond. I'm Mrs Crampsie. Come on into my study.
	Helen follows Mrs Crampsie.
Helen:	(*looking around*) What a pleasant room. I knew all the horrid stories about this place were untrue.
Mrs Crampsie:	You what, love?
Helen:	Oh, never mind. (*smiles*) A lovely room.
Mrs Crampsie:	Aye, 'tis an' all. Unusual name, Diamond.
Helen:	(*thinks*) Yes, I suppose so.
Mrs Crampsie:	My daughter married a Diamond, a long distance lorry driver, she don't see much of 'im. (*pause*) Wouldn't be a relation, I suppose? You know, your 'usband comin' from Cambridge an' all.
Helen:	(*puzzled*) No, I don't think my husband has any relations in Cambridge. He's from Kent originally. But…
Mrs Crampsie:	Oh well, make yourself at 'ome love. Me daughter's comin' round in a tick.
	Oliver shouts from outside in a strange 'posh' voice.
Oliver:	Hello, anyone there? Which bedroom do I want, old girl?
Mrs Crampsie:	(*shouts*) First on your right, top of the stairs. (*to Helen, who appears puzzled*) By the way, what's your Diamond do?
Helen:	Now, that's the funny…
	There is a crashing sound on the stairs, outside.
Oliver:	Ouch, ah, fiddlesticks! I've hurt my old foot. I'll just hobble up to the bedroom, old girl.
Helen:	(*in a stage whisper*) Why are you speaking in that ridiculous voice, Oliver?
Oliver:	Me? Strange voice? What, what, old girl? Ha, a joke!
Helen:	(*exasperated*) Go on upstairs – we need to talk.
	As Helen walks out of the room, Pauline enters.
Pauline:	Eeh, Mam, is that Diamond fella related to my Ollie?
Mrs Crampsie:	(*shakes her head*) I don't think so, Pauline love, he's one of those posh, stupid types. You wouldn't go for that type of man, love.
Pauline:	No, I wouldn't like an educated twit. My Ollie's alright, eh Mam?
Mrs Crampsie:	Good job 'e's a lorry driver, eh? Gives you three or four days of peace?
	They both laugh as Oliver enters the room.
Oliver:	(*in 'posh' accent*) Excuse me, Mrs Cramp… sie
	Pauline and Mrs Crampsie stare at Oliver.

Pauline:	What're you doin' back here, Ollie? I thought you were in Cambridge?
Mrs Crampsie:	By heck, what you puttin' on that silly accent for, you great soft twerp! You're as bad as that fella who's just arrived.
Oliver:	(*thinking quickly*) Well, you see, I heard this posh bloke upstairs, and er, and I thought I'd imitate him.
Pauline:	(*laughs a raucous laugh*) Oh, you are a one, Ollie!
	Enter Derek Mumford, an old friend of Oliver's, from Kent.
Derek:	(*to Oliver*) Saw your car outside, Oliver. Wondered what you were doing here.
Pauline:	(*to Derek*) He lives 'ere with me and me mam, of course!
Derek:	Well, actually, there must be some sort of a…
Oliver:	(*interrupting*) Derek, (*laughs*) can I have a quiet word?
	Oliver takes Derek to one side.
	I'm in a bit of a fix, and, er…
	Helen enters the room. She smiles at Oliver and links her arm through his.
Oliver:	Helen, what a coincidence! Let me introduce you to Derek Mumford. He…
Helen:	(*to Oliver*) I know who this man is. He's Mr Diamond. Mrs Crampsie has already told me. Isn't it an amazing coincidence, sweetie-pie?
Pauline:	(*to her mum*) That 'orrid Mrs Diamond has linked arms with my Ollie. Very forward, those southerners. Shall I hit 'er one?
Mrs Crampsie:	Oh Pauline, they're all like that down south, it's just their way. Take no notice, love.
Pauline:	(*to her mum*) 'Er husband looks a right drip!
Mrs Crampsie:	(*nodding*) I know, love. Good job you married Ollie.
Pauline:	(*shouts to Derek*) Hello, Mr Diamond.
Derek:	(*confused*) Why is everyone calling me Diamond? The name is Mumford.
	The three women speak in unison.
Pauline:	Mumford?
Mrs Crampsie:	Mumford?
Helen:	Mumford?
Oliver:	(*quickly*) Mumford-Diamond. (*nudges Derek*) Double-barrelled name, you know.
	The following rapid speech is spoken almost simultaneously.
Pauline:	Typical southerners!
Derek:	Don't keep nudging me, Oliver.
Mrs Crampsie:	Bet he's a crook. Never trust people with double-barrelled names.

Helen:	(*to Derek*) How do you know his (*indicates Derek*), how do you know his name, Oliver?
Derek:	(*to Oliver*) The reason I'm here is…
Oliver:	(*grabs Derek*) Go on?
Derek:	(*to Oliver*) Your wife Kirsty needs a break from her life in Kent. Seeing you once a month isn't on, you know. She's decided to have a weekend away from it all! I'm here to book her a room. She'll be here herself soon… isn't that a surprise, Oliver? A nice surprise for both of you, on your wedding anniversary.
Oliver:	(*resigned*) Er, yes, quite a surprise!
	He *faints*.
Pauline:	Ollie, my Ollie.
Helen:	Oliver, sweetie-pie!

Lesson Notes

Seated

In pairs or groups

Analysis of characters.

Take each character in turn. Discuss the main things you notice about each character in terms of the way they behave/speak/react to each other and then pinpoint the evidence in the text which shows this. Make a table like the one below:

Character	Points to notice	Evidence
Oliver	Makes frantic excuses	Says 'It's just that all the drivers tell me it's a... erm... dirty, dingy little place.'

Active

In groups

- Identify what you consider to be five key moments in the farce.
- Make up a title for each of these moments, as though each one is a snapshot photo with a headline.
- Compose the still-life photo (freeze-frame) to accompany each title.
- Perform them in sequence with one person speaking the title for each freeze frame.
- The teacher will ask one character in each freeze-frame to come to life and to voice what they are thinking at this moment in the action.

Written

Collect some leaflets advertising theatre productions. Examine the format and analyse the language that is used to persuade people to visit the show. Then, design your own theatre leaflet publicising *The Bigamist* with a brief description of the plot and reasons for going to see it.

Tragedy

A tragedy usually deals with a tragic hero – somebody whose fortune changes from happiness to misery, due to a character flaw or an error of judgement on that character's part. In Glen Stockdale's case, the flaw is his relentless ambition.

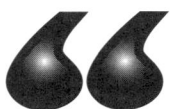 The Tragedy of Glen Stockdale

> **Characters**
> Glen Stockdale – ambitious member of parliament
> Alan Marshall – prime minister
> Ms Winters – home secretary
> David Noremac – friend of Glen Stockdale
> Old Lady 1 – clairvoyant
> Old Lady 2 – clairvoyant
> Old Lady 3 – clairvoyant
> Martha – Glen Stockdale's wife
> Dr Coles
> Terry Hammond – minister without portfolio
> Paper Boy
> Two Policemen – non-speaking parts

Inside Number 10 Downing Street, London.

Marshall: I think we must be prepared to lose this election, both of the opposition parties have united against us.

Ms Winters: (*entering – out of breath*) I am sure you are wrong, Prime Minister. You should have seen Glen Stockdale's attack on the other parties' policies during the live television debate. He was magnificent!

Marshall: But we are behind in the opinion polls and the election takes place tomorrow.

Ms Winters: Yes, but the very latest polls put us slightly ahead, after Glen Stockdale's tour of the inner cities and his television appearance.

Marshall: (*cheerful*) When I see him, I shall make him foreign secretary in our new administration.

Out in the streets in a blustery November gale, Glen Stockdale and his loyal friend, David Noremac, are canvassing the public.

Stockdale: Well, my friend, we shall win the election yet!

Noremac:	Yes, and Marshall will thank us. Loyalty to the party is everything to him.
	Three old ladies, carrying shopping bags walk past the two politicians.
Old Lady 1:	Glen Stockdale, minister of education.
Old Lady 2:	Glen Stockdale, foreign secretary.
Old Lady 3:	Glen Stockdale, prime minister of the future.
Stockdale:	What? I am the minister of education, but why address me as foreign secretary or prime minister?
	The three old ladies dash off and jump on a bus that quickly pulls away.
Noremac:	Don't take any notice, Glen. They're just three barmy old women.
Stockdale:	(*laughs*) Foreign secretary, indeed!
	Stockdale's mobile phone rings.
Ms Winters:	(*on her mobile*) Oh, Glen… just to give you a bit of news. Marshall likes you so much he's going to make you foreign secretary if we win the election.
Stockdale:	(*shocked*) Were those three old ladies speaking the truth?
Ms Winters:	(*narrating*) The government won the election by a larger majority than expected. Glen Stockdale was made foreign secretary. Later, he was reunited with his wife.
Martha:	(*to Glen*) Are you happy with your new position, Glen? You could be so much more, my dear. The people like you, your party adores you. You won the election for old Alan Marshall and you know he's a fool!
Stockdale:	(*kisses wife*) What can I do? He's not going to resign and the old ladies tell me I should be prime minister one day.
Martha:	(*frowns*) One day? Why not now? All you need to do is 'phone the press and tell them about Marshall's affair with that attractive secretary of his. What's her name… Roxanne Dart.
Stockdale:	No… I couldn't… it would destroy Marshall, and he's such a good man.
Martha:	(*picks up telephone*) Do it for our sake. You deserve the highest office, you know you do. As your loving wife, I'll make a great hostess at Number 10.
Stockdale:	(*relenting*) Are you sure this will work?
Martha:	(*bright*) It can't fail! (*hands telephone to Glen*) Go on, ring the press barons and finish Marshall.
	A week later, Glen Stockdale is prime minister. He is at Number 10 with the minister without portfolio, Terry Hammond.
Stockdale:	I worry about David Noremac. After all, he was with me when the three old ladies gave me the idea of being prime minister.
Hammond:	(*thoughtful*) The public don't like Noremac. After his attempts to stop

the spread of infantile pneumonia in sheep by destroying the lambs, the press have nicknamed him Herod.

Both men laugh heartily.

Stockdale:	Noremac might be as ambitious as me and try to take my job. He knows too much about me. Ring the secret service, we shall dispose of Noremac! A simple job of fixing the brakes in his car.
Paper Boy:	Read all about it, read all about it, death of agricultural secretary, David Noremac, in car smash on M4.
Martha:	Glen, you've gone too far. Too far. How could you have engineered his death? David's been your friend since university days.
Stockdale:	(*hisses*) I am the most popular prime minister for an entire generation. Don't tell me what to do.
Martha:	(*crying*) I wish you'd never become prime minister.
Stockdale:	And who's bright idea was that, eh? Well, now I have power, I intend to use it. (*roughly*) So, out of my way Martha!

Three years later. Glen Stockdale is looking through the morning papers, at Number 10. The news is not good, and Martha, his wife, appears unhappy. Stockdale picks up his mobile and dials.

Hammond? See me immediately!

Martha leaves in tears as Tony Hammond enters.

Ms Joan Winters is a threat. I need her disposed of at once!

Hammond:	You'll never pin anything on our home secretary. She's wholesome and clean-living.
Stockdale:	(*impatient*) Arrange a multiple pile-up on the M25, Hammond. Do something! I want her dead!
Paper Boy:	Read all about it. Miracle escape from accident by home secretary, Joan Winters.
Stockdale:	(*annoyed*) Winters should be dead, Hammond, dead!
Hammond:	(*apologetic*) She's as good as dead, prime minister. With her injuries, she'll be in hospital for months.

Dr Coles bursts into the room.

Dr Coles:	Excuse me, prime minister, your wife – she's had a complete nervous breakdown.
Stockdale:	(*impatient*) Well, cure her then, you're a doctor, cure her.

Dr Coles rushes out of the room. Martha cries out, off-stage. There is silence.

Dr Coles:	(*returning*) Excuse me, prime minister.

The telephone rings, Terry Hammond answers the phone.

Stockdale:	(*to himself*) I have grown tired of this politics game. I enjoyed playing when I was climbing the ladder of success. In fact, I was very

ambitious, but now I know everyone is against me, they all want me to resign! The problem was, I wanted to be prime minister at all costs. (*laughs bitterly*) I hadn't even thought out any clear policies.

Hammond: (*replacing the receiver*) The party chairman Lord Kershaw has just informed me the latest opinion polls put us 20 points behind the opposition.

Dr Coles: (*apologetic*) Your wife, Mr Stockdale, is dead. Suicide.

Stockdale: (*sadly*) Take away her body, arrange a funeral. I loved her once, but not now. I shall mourn later.

Ms Winters staggers into the room on crutches. Behind her are two armed policemen.

Ah, Ms Winters, I am so glad you recovered from your nasty accident.

Ms Winters: (*coldly*) I took the liberty of bugging your office – with the help of Terry Hammond.

Stockdale: (*shocked*) What? Hammond, you double-crossing…

Hammond: What the lady says is true.

Ms Winters: (*to Stockdale*) I want your resignation letter now; for the sake of the party, you understand. I shall inform the Commons that our party is to pick a new leader as soon as possible. (*pause*) You had great potential, Stockdale, your tragedy is, you were consumed by ambition.

Stockdale is led away by the two armed policemen. As Ms Winters and Terry Hammond walk out of Number 10, they are approached by three old ladies.

Lesson Notes

Seated

In pairs

Devise questions you would ask of the actor playing Glen Stockdale about how he created the character for the stage.

You might like to consider the following:

● What are Glen Stockdale's motives?
● Does Glen Stockdale have any particular strengths or weaknesses?
● How did the actor get into role? Were there any parts that were difficult to perform?
● Does the actor have a personal opinion of the issues raised in the script such as political ambition, personal gain or the hunger for power?

Active

Experimenting with status

Status can be described as the rank or importance which other people consider you to have. Status is constructed socially, or, in other words, it is only made up of other people's opinions of your importance/wealth/position/fame/personality. How we behave towards other people is dependent on whether we think they are of higher, lower or the same status as ourselves. For example, consider how you speak to someone of higher status (e.g. a celebrity or your headteacher) in comparison to how you talk to someone you consider to be of lower status than yourself (e.g. an irritating younger brother or sister) or someone of the same status (e.g. a friend).

● In large groups (of 7 or 8), the teacher will choose one person to be the high status individual. Everyone else must treat this person like royalty – perhaps even carrying her/him from place to place, physically. All of the 'servers' bow down before the high status person and flatter him/her while carrying out lots of small duties.
● The high status person in each group should report back at the end of the exercise on how this made them feel.
● Consider how this links in with what happens to Glen Stockdale.

Written

Persuasive writing

Look at examples of political advertising and identify the techniques used to try to influence the reader.

Design a poster and a political leaflet for Stockdale's party using some of the techniques you have identified.

Scenarios with Citizenship

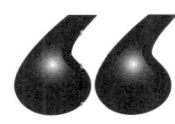 King Xerxes' Power

> **Characters**
> Narrator
> King Xerxes – a powerful king and absolute ruler
> Queen Vashti – a strong-minded queen
> Frank – a noble
> Malcolm – a noble
> Haman – an evil man with dark desires to control the king
> Suzanne – servant to Queen Vashti
> Colette – servant to Queen Vashti
> Michael – an old foreigner with sense and wisdom
> Esther – a wise and beautiful young woman
> Soldier 1
> Soldier 2
> Barry – a would-be assassin
> Terry – another would-be assassin
> Zara – wife of Haman and an evil influence

Scene One

Inside King Xerxes' palace.

Narrator:	A long time ago, in a different country to our own, there lived a rich and powerful king.
King:	I have conquered three countries and I intend to make war against three more.
Narrator:	To make things easier, I have changed the names of some of the characters in this play because you would have trouble pronouncing some of them. Although I would not dare change the name of the great King Xerxes.
King:	Nobody ever pronounces my name correctly – it's Xerxes. But you may call me king; as powerful a king and as mighty a ruler as there ever was!
Narrator:	Getting back to the story – the great and powerful king had been on his throne for three years. In that short time he had won great victories.
King:	(*to his nobles*) So, I want to show off. I intend to hold a great banquet

that will last for seven days. I'll hold the banquet in our beautiful garden. I shall serve the wine in golden goblets. Each man may drink as much wine as he wants.

Frank:	Yes, your royal highness, as your majesty commands.
Queen:	(*entering the palace and bowing before the king*) I have heard about the banquet, my dear husband. May I hold one for the women, so that they, too, can see the glory of your palace?
King:	(*quickly*) Yes, yes, of course, Queen Vashti.
Narrator:	Six days later, the king and his nobles are drinking wine from the golden goblets.
King:	(*thoughtful*) I have shown off everything I have in the kingdom.
Malcolm:	(*bows*) You have, my lord. We have even seen the maps, showing all the countries your majesty has conquered.
Haman:	We have seen your beautiful palace and colourful mosaics, we have seen all you have, all your wealth and power, oh mighty ruler. (*to himself*) All this makes me so jealous!
Frank:	We all know your greatness, oh king.
King:	(*thoughtful*) You have seen it all, except my queen. She is the most beautiful woman in all the land. (*impulsive*) Malcolm, you must fetch her here, at once. I need to show off my queen.

Malcolm hurries off to fetch the queen.

Scene Two

The queen's banquet.

Queen:	No doubt my husband is blind drunk. Well, we girls can have a swim in the heated pool. The palace has its luxuries!
Suzanne:	We're picking up a fine suntan.
Colette:	The grapes are delicious!

Enter Malcolm.

Queen:	(*shocked*) What are you doing in the ladies' quarters, Malcolm? (*quickly*) Fetch me my robe, Colette.
Malcolm:	(*embarrassed*) Er, I beg your pardon, your majesty, but the king commands your presence.
Queen:	(*offended*) He promised he wouldn't disturb my banquet.
Malcolm:	He has commanded…
Queen:	Yes, yes… But I need to dress for the occasion. I'm only wearing my swimsuit.
Malcolm:	Oh queen, he wants to see you straight away, without delay.
Suzanne:	(*to Vashti*) He intends to show you off to all the nobles, he wants you to display your lovely figure to them all. It boosts his ego, isn't that

	right, Malcolm?
	Malcolm nods.
Queen:	(*angry*) Tell Xerxes he can wait. I'm not a toy he can pick up and put down at will. Now go!
	Malcolm runs off.
Colette:	Your majesty, you have acted hastily. The king will be furious.
Suzanne:	There may be terrible consequences, your majesty.
Queen:	(*laughs*) He adores me. He wouldn't do anything to harm me.

Scene Three

	The king's palace.
Narrator:	Malcolm relates all that has happened. King Xerxes is very angry.
King:	How dare the queen defy me! What shall I do? What does the law permit me to do? Give me advice, now!
	The king wanders off to refill his wine glass.
Haman:	Quick, men – the king wants a decision. (*to himself*) I'll give him a decision that will bring about the queen's destruction. She never did like me!
Frank:	(*to Haman*) I don't know what the law permits and I can't be bothered to find out. I've drunk too much wine, I can't think straight.
Haman:	Listen boys, this is what we'll do… (*he sees the king returning*). Just leave it all to me.
King:	What does one do when one's wife is disobedient?
Malcolm:	The queen has done wrong…
King:	(*quickly*) Yes, she most certainly has.
Haman:	… and the queen's conduct will become known to all women. They will all disobey their husbands as the queen has disobeyed you.
King:	True!
Haman:	There will be disrespect and disloyalty throughout the great kingdom.
King:	Yes, there will!
Haman:	If it pleases the king… issue a royal decree, declaring that your wife Queen Vashti be banned from the kingdom.
King:	(*upset*) But, she's beautiful, I like her!
Haman:	Then give her position to somebody who is better than her. When the king's edict is proclaimed throughout your ever-growing kingdom, all women will respect their husbands – from the lowest to the greatest!
King:	Yes, I like the idea! Very well, round up all the beautiful women you can find. I'll choose the one I want.
Haman:	At once, your majesty.

King:	Oh, and banish Vashti, the former queen. I never want to see her again.
Haman:	(*smirks*) With pleasure, your majesty.

Scene Four

The home of a foreigner, Michael. The room is small.

Narrator:	Michael is cooking a meal. A beautiful young woman enters.
Michael:	Good evening, Esther, my dear.
Esther:	I wish we could go back to our own country, Father.
Michael:	We have no country, Esther. Our country lies in ruins. Only the vultures and the wild cats live there now… the pack dogs feed on the carcasses of our friends. The king and his army destroyed our country.
Esther:	So, we shall never see our home again.
Michael:	One day, perhaps, our ancestors will inhabit our country again – but not us, Esther, not us!
Esther:	Father…
Michael:	(*sadly*) Remember Esther, I am not your father. Your parents are dead… but I am proud that you call me father.

Soldiers burst into the little room.

Soldier 1:	In the name of King Xerxes, stand to attention.
Soldier 2:	(*glances at Esther*) She'll do.
Soldier 1:	But she's a foreigner.
Soldier 2:	Did the king say anything about foreigners? She's a beauty. She'll do.
Soldier 1:	Seize her!

Soldier 2 seizes Esther, who does not struggle.

Michael:	(*shocked*) What is the meaning of this outrage?
Soldier 2:	Out of my way, old man.

The soldier leads Esther away.

Michael:	(*sobs*) Will there be no end to our troubles?

Scene Five

The king's palace.

Narrator:	A month later, Malcolm presents Esther to the king.
King:	(*admires Esther*) Yes, you are beautiful. How would you like to be my wife?
Esther:	(*bows her head*) If it is your will, my lord.
King:	(*happy*) Obedience – the girl is obedient! Yes, you will make a good queen. We shall marry immediately.

	Soldier 1 leaves the palace and spots old Michael.
Soldier 1:	Old man, you cannot enter this palace. King Xerxes is to marry today. We shall have a new queen – Queen Esther.
	Old Michael walks slowly away. He sits down on a bench near the palace walls.
	He overhears a conversation.
Barry:	(*angry*) This King Xerxes deserves to die. He banished my cousin Vashti and he refused to make me captain of the guards.
Terry:	I've a grudge against him, too. He did not promote me to the royal household after the last battle – and I would have fought bravely if I hadn't been in bed with a fever.
Barry:	We are resolved to assassinate the king as he leaves the royal palace!
	They both draw their swords.
Terry:	Haman will take over as king, then we shall receive honours!
Narrator:	Michael, hearing all, hurried off to tell Frank and Malcolm the plot. The king was saved. However, the king did not want to know all the details of the conspiracy against him.
King:	(*to Malcolm*) That old man, Michael, is brave! Record all that he has done for me.
Frank:	What shall we do with the two villains, your majesty? (*to himself*) Haman will see me honoured one day. I will not mention his implication in the plot.
King:	Hang the two villains!
	Barry and Terry are led to the gallows.
Esther:	(*to herself*) The king must not know old Michael is my stepfather.
Haman:	(*watches old Michael shuffle away*) Foreigners! That old Michael saved the king's life. He refuses to bow down to me. though. I hate him!
	Haman runs to the King's side.
	There are certain people mixing with our kinsmen who have different customs to us. They do not fully obey our laws. These are the people we have conquered, but they are spoiling our own race.
King:	(*shocked*) Oh dear – well Haman, what do you suggest we do about it?
Haman:	Round up all these foreigners and have them killed. They won't help us when we invade new territories, they'll be our enemies within!
King:	Indeed? Well, do as you wish Haman, I am too busy to be bothered with such trifling matters.
Haman:	As I wish? (*bows*) As your majesty decrees!
	Haman smiles as he walks towards the soldiers.
Narrator:	When old Michael discovers what is to happen to him and his people, he asks Queen Esther to help. She approaches the king and asks him

to hold a banquet for the two of them, and Haman.

King:	A strange request, but how could one refuse? Esther has been a good and loyal wife.

Scene Six

In their large family home, Haman boasts to his wife.

Zara:	You seem very happy tonight, my husband.
Haman:	I have great wealth, many sons and a loving wife. Why shouldn't I be happy? I have also persuaded the king to kill all these foreigners that infest our land. Including old Michael, the man who uncovered the assassination attempt on King Xerxes.
Zara:	Why are you jealous of old Michael?
Haman:	I want to be the only man the king likes. I am, you know, number two in the kingdom.
Zara:	(*an evil thought crosses her mind*) Have a gallows built seventy-five feet high, and ask King Xerxes to have old Michael hanged on it!
Haman:	I shall ask the king tonight, when I dine with just him and the queen. They both think so much of me that I'm the only person invited to dine with the royalty.
Zara:	Oh, Haman – I'm so proud of you!
Narrator:	But pride comes before a fall, as we all know.

Scene Seven

Narrator:	At the palace, the king paced up and down his room. He felt uneasy.
King:	(*to Frank*) Go get the great book of chronicles. Read about the assassination attempt last year. Who uncovered the plot to kill me?
Frank:	An old man, the foreigner Michael.
King:	What honour and recognition did I bestow on Michael the foreigner?
Frank:	None, my lord.
	Haman enters. The king escorts Haman to the banquet. Queen Esther is at the table, waiting.
King:	Ah, Haman, what recognition should one bestow on a man who has shown great loyalty and honour?
Haman:	(*to himself*) At last! He is talking about me… (*to the king*) Give this man a robe you have worn and a horse you have ridden. Let me, er… let this man ride through the city streets so that all who see him know that he is your number two.
King:	Yes – now what should one do to a man that cannot be trusted?
Haman:	That man, oh wise ruler, must die at the gallows. I have prepared

gallows for such a man!

King:	It shall be done.
Queen:	(*interrupting*) Old Michael is my stepfather. He raised me and looked after me. He is a kind and generous old man. I am a foreigner. If he and his people die, I must die too!
King:	Now don't upset yourself, Esther. Your stepfather will wear my cloak and ride my horse. Haman, it is you who will hang on the gallows. (*shouts*) Guards! Arrest Haman! (*to Esther*) From now on, I shall consult my queen before making any decisions. I have not been myself in the past. From now on, I shall rule wisely. Your people shall be free to do as they please for as long as I reign!

Lesson Notes

Seated

Storyboard the section in the play where Queen Vashti refuses to see the king and she is banished from the kingdom.

Active

Improvise and act out the scene where Haman is sent to the gallows.

Written

List the qualities you think a good leader should have and, on the basis of this, write a speech persuading your year group that you should be elected leader of your student council.

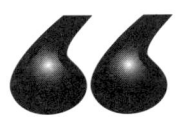 ## Josh's Weekend Away

Characters
Josh – a boy from Springdown Meadows, a residential home
Heidi – a helper at Springdown Meadows
Melvin – another boy from Springdown Meadows
Mr Doyle
Mrs Doyle
Stephanie Doyle – daughter of Mr and Mrs Doyle
Kevin Doyle – spoilt son of Mr and Mrs Doyle

Josh is packing his bag, stuffing his favourite video and his football boots into his bag and attempting to fasten the zip. Heidi walks into his small bedroom.

Heidi:	Are you nervous, Josh?
Josh:	Nervous? Me?
Heidi:	You're only staying with the Doyle family for a weekend, Josh – not six months.
Josh:	I know, but I might need all the stuff I've put in my bag. I'd better take everything just in case.
Heidi:	I hope it all works out for you, Josh. If anyone deserves to get away from here, it's you. You need to be with a family. The home doesn't suit your needs any longer.
Josh:	(*bites his lip*) Do you think they'll like me, Heidi?

Heidi pauses and thinks.

Heidi:	I've seen too many of you disappointed, Josh. It isn't easy fitting into an established family. (*she grins*) But, in all my years working at Springdown, I've never known a boy deserve a family as much as you do. Good luck!

Heidi ruffles Josh's hair. Both are embarrassed by this unexpected burst of affection.

Josh:	(*shy*) Thanks, Heidi.

As Heidi leaves the room, Melvin enters. He is a tall, muscular boy with a sour look about him.

Melvin:	Going away?
Josh:	Yeah, I've got a weekend with a family.

Melvin:	(*sarcastic*) Bet that'll be fun, Josh.
Josh:	(*quiet*) I hope so.
Melvin:	(*loud*) I hope so! Give me a break. They won't want you and you won't want them. Those of us who live here, we're different.
Josh:	(*shrugs his shoulders*) Well, you never know!
Melvin:	We've both been here for too long. Families have kind of romantic ideas about fostering us. Then something goes wrong and, as soon as it does, back we come to Springdown Meadows – you'll see. I've been there, done that. I know what I'm talking about.
Josh:	Sure. Thanks for the confidence boost, Melvin. Great reassurance.
Melvin:	(*nasty*) That's OK. Anything for a pal.

Much later, Josh is sitting in the Doyle family living room. He has been introduced to the family. Stephanie is older than Josh, and she appears friendly. Kevin is about Josh's age. He is quite resentful.

Mrs Doyle:	You'll share a room with Kevin, Joshua, but it's a big bedroom with plenty of space.
Kevin:	(*sulky*) Mum, does he have to share with me?

Kevin prods Josh in the chest.

Mr Doyle:	Shhh, Kevin! It's only for the weekend.
Stephanie:	(*bright*) Come and look around the house, Joshua. I'll show you everything, including the cellar, where Kevin keeps all his old baby toys.
Kevin:	(*angry*) You wait, Steph. I'll show him a photo of you in the nude on Brighton beach when you were two years old.
Mrs Doyle:	Now, now you two. I'll start the cooking. We have our main meal at six o'clock, Joshua.
Stephanie:	(*to Josh*) She likes us to be on time! Come on Joshua, I'll show you all the secrets of the house.
Josh:	Um, nobody ever calls me Joshua at the home. (*shyly*) It's Josh, if that's alright with you?
Stephanie:	(*laughs*) Oh relax! Josh is fine. By the way, what did happen to your mum and dad? (*silence*) Sorry, I shouldn't have asked that – I'm just nosy.
Josh:	That's alright, Stephanie.
Stephanie:	(*relieved*) Cool.
Josh:	I don't know who my dad was – I don't know if he's dead or alive – but mum had me when she was very young. She was fifteen.
Stephanie:	Wow! I'm fifteen now and I'm definitely not responsible enough to have a baby.
Josh:	Mum couldn't cope, so my grandma looked after me. When I was eight, she took ill and died. That's when I was sent to Springdown Meadows. I've been there ever since – almost four years now.

Stephanie:	Oh, I'm so sorry.
Josh:	My mum met a Greek fellow called Spiros. She lives in Kefalonia – one of the Greek islands. She doesn't want me with her. I don't even know what she looks like, not really. Gran had some old photos, but Mum will be about twenty-eight now.
Stephanie:	Mum and Dad think Kevin is spoilt. A brother about his age would do him good. (*whispers*) Play your cards right, and you could become part of the family.
	Kevin creeps up behind Stephanie.
Kevin:	I bet she hasn't shown you the sick stain on the carpet, when she didn't make it to the bathroom last month.
Stephanie:	(*embarrassed*) Kevin!
Kevin:	She'd been to her boyfriend's party and…
Josh:	(*quickly*) Could I see your room, Kevin?
Kevin:	You can see my room, yeah.
	Kevin shows Josh the large bedroom.
Kevin:	I've got a lot of things and they take up most of the room. I've squeezed you in by the window. Mum's made up a camp bed.
Josh:	(*disappointed*) Oh.
Kevin:	(*pointedly*) Seeing as you're only here for the one weekend.
Josh:	(*looking around the room*) Wow, you support Southampton. That's a coincidence, so do I!
Kevin:	(*brightening*) Really?
Josh:	Matt Howlett's the best centre forward in the game.
Kevin:	You're dead right there!
	Kevin grabs a football from the corner of his bedroom.
	Do you play?
Josh:	Yeah, we have two teams at the home.
Kevin:	Let's have a kick-around outside.
	Josh follows Kevin down into the garden.
	We'll have a goal each end of the garden. We'll be goalkeepers and forwards. Whoever scores ten first is the winner. Right?
Josh:	(*laughs*) Right!
	Kevin takes the ball and dribbles past Josh. He shoots and misses. Josh take the ball, runs and scores. From then on, Josh scores again – and again.
Kevin:	(*annoyed*) You're too good for me!
Josh:	Not really, just luck!

Josh allows Kevin to run past him and score.

Kevin: 3-1! Chance for a come back – just like Southampton did last week.

Kevin misses, kicking the ball so that it flies off, at an angle, crashing through the lounge window. There is a splintering of glass.

Kevin: Oh no, Mum will kill me.

Mrs Doyle: (*breathless*) What's happened? Kevin, tell me what's going on.

Kevin: It's the boy from the home. He kicked the ball at the window, deliberately. I saw him do it.

Josh: (*upset*) That's not true. (*points to Kevin*) He broke the window!

Kevin: (*to Mrs Doyle*) Who do you believe, Mum me or a stranger? He broke the window!

Josh: (*to himself*) What did Melvin tell me? I was a fool to build up my hopes.

Lesson Notes

Seated

Hot-Seating

Try to recall as many facts as possible. In groups of three or four, hot-seat the following characters:

- **Josh**

  What were his hopes and fears concerning his weekend away?

  What are his hopes and fears now?

- **Mrs Doyle**

  What did she wish for and how have her plans worked out?

- **Kevin**

  Why is Kevin so against Josh?

  What are his reasons and motivations for being so dishonest?

- **Stephanie**

  Why does Stephanie want Josh to stay?

  What does she think of Josh and what does she think of Kevin?

  What can she say to her parents to persuade them that Josh ought to be part of the family?

Active

Thought-tracking

Thought-tracking allows the character to speak his/her true thoughts or feelings at any point in the script. After reading the script aloud once, the seven characters who have performed should stand in the centre of a circle formed by the remainder of the class. The audience in the outer circle should consider carefully the important moments in the script where interesting thoughts could be revealed. The seven performers recommence the performance and anyone from the outer circle can enter the centre and gently tap whoever is speaking, or any of the other characters, on the shoulder. At this point, all of the other characters freeze and the person who has been tapped takes one step backwards and begins to speak his/her true thoughts or feelings aloud. The performance continues when the character takes one step forward back into the inner circle.

Written

Continue to write the script of the play. How does it finish? You may wish to use ideas from the hot-seating or thought-tracking activities above.

Pre-1914 Text

Wilkie Collins, a famous writer of many pre-twentieth century novels, dealt with some unusual subjects and he allowed coincidence to play a part in many of his works. The script below is an adaptation of one of Collins' most popular short stories.

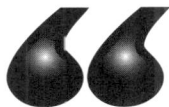 The Dead Hand

Characters
Mr James Holliday — a rich businessman
Arthur Holliday — his son
Dr Rook — a family friend
Porter
Innkeeper
Man with knapsack
Landlord — a money-grabbing man with a nasty
    sense of humour
Dead Man

It is the autumn of 1844 and Mr Holliday is talking to his son, Arthur, in Mr Holliday's study.

Mr H: Oh yes, Arthur, do visit the racecourse in Doncaster. How can I stop you spending money and enjoying yourself when I myself was rather wild, in my youth?

Arthur: Yes, Father, you have already told me something of your past.

Mr H: Unlike most parents, I am not going to be angry if I find you take after me (*he hands Arthur a bag of money*). No, indeed no (*chuckles to himself*). Rather the reverse. I wish I could bring back some of the good old days (*coughs*). Too late though now, Arthur. I'm too old for enjoying the races. Get to Doncaster and enjoy yourself, as I once did!

Arthur: Thank you, Father.

              Some time later. Arthur is on the train to Doncaster, seated next to a middle-aged gentleman.

Dr Rook: You off to the races, young man?

Arthur: (*enthusiastic*) Yes, indeed!

Dr Rook: Are you any relation of Mr James Holliday, the rich manufacturer?

Arthur: (*startled*) Why yes, yes I am!

Dr Rook:	(*laughs*) You're the image of your father, young man. I knew James in his younger days, before he made his fortune. (*laughs*) What a rake he was – oh, pardon me. (*pause*) But I do hope you do not take after your father.
Arthur:	(*indignant*) No sir, I do not! I am engaged to be married.
Dr Rook:	Not a chip off the old block, eh? Well, I hope you find accommodation in Doncaster. Life here is hectic and many places are full during the racing season (*he digs into his waistcoat pocket*). Here is my card, should you need my help (*Arthur takes Dr Rook's card*). And regards to your father. He will remember me – Charles Rook. (*stands up*) I believe we're in Doncaster now.
	Arthur follows Dr Rook onto the platform and addresses the porter.
Arthur:	Can you recommend a place I could stay in Doncaster?
Porter:	Aye, I could, but not this week. Don't you know it's race week? You wouldn't get a place to stay round here, not now you won't.
	Arthur is crestfallen. He wanders the main street of Doncaster and knocks at many inn doors. Mime Arthur knocking on doors and innkeepers shaking their heads.
Innkeeper:	(*cross*) What d'yer want?
Arthur:	(*uncertain*) I was rather… hoping… you had a vacancy.
Innkeeper:	Oh aye? Not this week. It's race week.
Man with knapsack:	Looking for a place, are you, young man?
Arthur:	Yes, yes I am. I've tried all over town. No luck!
Man with knapsack:	Try The Two Robins, just around the corner. It's a bit on the seedy side, but you could be in luck.
Arthur:	Thanks.
	Arthur rushes off.
Man with knapsack:	(*to innkeeper*) Old Bill, the landlord, never turns a customer away.
	At The Two Robins
Arthur:	(*to landlord*) If you have a bed to let, I'll pay you good money (*jingles his pockets*).
Landlord:	Will you offer me a really good price?
Arthur:	Name your price – and I'll give you the money. At once, if you like?
Landlord:	(*greedy*) Are you game for five shillings?
Arthur:	(*takes out a bag of money*) Here (*counts*). Five shillings. It's raining and I need a bed for the night.
Landlord:	(*looks hard at Arthur*) You're acting all fair and above board and before I take your money, I'll do the same by you.

Arthur:	(*hopeful*) So, I'll get a bed?
Landlord:	(*thoughtful*) Look here, this is how it stands. You can have a bed all to yourself for five shillings, but you can't have more than a half-share of the room it stands in. Understand, young gentleman?
Arthur:	(*annoyed*) You mean it's a twin-bedded room, and one of the beds is occupied?

The landlord nods his head. The rain falls in torrents.

Landlord:	Is it yes or no? Settle quick, there are others who will want a bed in Doncaster tonight.

Arthur nods his head. The landlord and Arthur walk into the inn.

Arthur:	What sort of a man has got the other bed? Is he a gentleman? (*anxious*) Is he a quiet, well-behaved person?
Landlord:	(*chuckles*) He's the quietest man I ever came across. As sober as a judge, as regular as clockwork in his habits. It's not yet nine in the evening and he's already abed.
Arthur:	(*curious*) Is he asleep, do you think?
Landlord:	(*chuckles*) I know he's asleep and I guarantee you won't wake him. Now follow me, sir… after you've paid.

Arthur hands over the five shillings. The landlord lights two candles.

Come and see the room, sir.

They walk up a flight of stairs and stand outside the room.

I warrant you won't be interfered with, or annoyed in any way.

They walk into a large, clean room. The occupied bed is near a large window Arthur peers at the man in the bed.

Arthur:	(*concerned*) He's a very quiet sleeper.
Landlord:	(*jolly*) Yes, very quiet.
Arthur:	The man is very pale.
Landlord:	Yes, pale enough isn't he?

Arthur walks over to the bed and inspects the man.

Arthur:	(*steps back, shocked*) He's not asleep. He's dead!
Landlord:	(*backs out of the room*) You've found that out sooner than I thought you would. He died at five o'clock this evening. Heart attack, no doubt. The Coroner's inquest starts tomorrow. Doctor's seen him. He's most certainly dead. (*smug*) You don't expect your five shillings back, do you? There's the empty bed I promised you.

The Landlord points to the empty bed.

I've kept my side of the bargain and I mean to keep the money (*laughs*).

Arthur:	(*angry*) Don't laugh – you shan't have my five shillings for nothing. (*rash*) I shall keep my bed, be there a dead man in the room or be there not.

Landlord:	(*laughs*) Have a good night's rest!
	Arthur takes the candle and walks over to his bed. The candle blows out, but a full moon illuminates the dead man's bed. The rain has stopped.
Arthur:	(*to himself*) It's but a few hours. I can get away first thing in the morning.
	He sits on his bed.
	Poor fellow. Ah, poor fellow!
	The 'dead' man's hand moves and flops down at the side of the bed.
	Did I hear a noise?
	There is a groan from the 'dead' man.
	He moved!
	Arthur rushes to the door, shouting.
	Landlord! Landlord!
	The landlord rushes up the stairs with a lighted candle.
Landlord:	Why disturb the peace, young fellow?
Arthur:	(*afraid*) The dead man moved!
	There is a groan from the bed.
Landlord:	(*alarmed*) I'll fetch the doctor.
Arthur:	No, no, (*searches in his pocket for Doctor Rook's card*) I'll pay for a doctor, a good man, a friend of the family. Fetch Doctor Rook!
	Arthur sits beside the 'dead' man's bed while he waits for Doctor Rook, who arrives after a short while and examines the 'dead' man. The man groans every now and then.
Landlord:	(*apologetic*) He was dead at five this evening.
Dr Rook:	(*sympathetic*) It does happen. A man may appear dead but it has been known for a man to wake up in his coffin, even after he's buried below ground. The heart is a funny thing, it can restart – occasionally!
Landlord:	He's coming round.
Dead Man:	Oh, have I been ill?
Landlord:	You could say that, yes.
Dr Rook:	(*to the 'dead' man*) You have been ill. Mr Holliday here has saved your life. He sent for me at his expense.
Dead Man:	(*shocked*) Holliday?
Arthur:	Arthur Holliday (*kindly*) and Doctor Rook.
Dead Man:	Doctor Rook? (*to the doctor*) Can I speak to you, alone?
Arthur:	(*to landlord*) Come on, let us leave this poor man to the doctor.
Landlord:	(*softening*) You did a good thing, saving that poor man's life. You may sleep in the basement tonight. I'll have a bed made up for you.

They leave the room.

Dead Man: (*to Dr Rook*) Do you think I look like Arthur Holliday? Have you noticed a certain resemblance?

Dr Rook: (*blunt*) Yes, and I know exactly who you are. You are Mr Holliday's illegitimate son. I was once a friend of the Hollidays. Your half-brother just saved your life.

Dead Man: But he must never know who I am, or what my name is, or his father – my father – won't pay me the small allowance I do receive from him. Mr James Holliday's legitimate son must never know I exist!

Dr Rook: Quite so.

Dead Man: I am a poor medical student, fallen on hard times.

Dr Rook: (*pleasant*) Yes, I suggested to James that you train for medicine (*smiles*). I have a large practice and I'm growing old. When you are better, seek me out. I need a partner (*hands 'dead' man his card*). Now don't worry, after a good meal and some rest, you will be well again.

Dr Rook steps forward, to face the audience.

And he *did* recover. He worked long, hard hours at my surgery. He became an excellent doctor, saving many lives. Arthur Holliday never did know he'd saved the life of his illegitimate half-brother that wild and wet night in Doncaster!

Lesson Notes

Seated

In pairs

Take the section from *Arthur: If you have a bed to let…* to the end.

- Focus on the creation of atmosphere in performance, bringing the text alive and making full sense of mystery/suspense/anticipation.
- Read through the section looking for external sound effects and tone of voice. Concentrate on the landlord and the clues given in what he says, but more importantly, how he says it and the double meanings implied. Consider lighting, props and facial expression.
- Discuss and note down all these elements, which contribute to the suspense. Then perform in your pairs, concentrating particularly on tone of voice and facial expression to convey atmosphere.

Active

In pairs

Freeze-frame specific moments from the text (look at the focal point of each picture and construct it as though you were planning a painting).

- Mr Holliday gives Arthur a bag of money.
- Landlord and Arthur – *Landlord: (greedy) Are you game for five shillings?*
- Landlord and Arthur – *Arthur: He's not asleep. He's dead!*
- Landlord and Arthur – *Arthur: Shame on you!*
- Landlord and Arthur – *Arthur: The dead man moved!*
- Dead Man and Dr Rook – *Dead Man: Do you think I look like Arthur Holliday?*

Written

Write the next scene when Dr Rook tells his story to a news reporter years later, after Arthur Holliday's father has died.

Original Material

Pride and Prejudice

A novel by Jane Austen, published in 1813.

Chapter One

It is a truth universally acknowledged, that a single man in possession of a good fortune, must be in want of a wife.

However little known the feelings or views of such a man may be on his first entering a neighbourhood, this truth is so well fixed in the minds of the surrounding families, that he is considered as the rightful property of some one or other of their daughters.

'My dear Mr Bennet,' said his lady to him one day, 'have you heard that Netherfield Park is let at last?'

Mr Bennet replied that he had not.

'But it is,' returned she; 'for Mrs Long has just been here, and she told me all about it.'

Mr Bennet made no answer.

'Do not you want to know who has taken it?' cried his wife impatiently.

'You want to tell me, and I have no objection to hearing it.'

This was invitation enough.

'Why, my dear, you must know, Mrs Long says that Netherfield is taken by a young man of large fortune from the north of England; that he came down on Monday in a chaise and four to see the place, and was so much delighted with it that he agreed with Mr Morris immediately; that he is to take possession before Michaelmas, and some of his servants are to be in the house by the end of next week.'

'What is his name?'

'Bingley.'

'Is he married or single?'

'Oh! Single, my dear, to be sure! A single man of large fortune; four or five thousand a year. What a fine thing for our girls!'

'How so? How can it affect them?'

'My dear Mr Bennet,' replied his wife, 'how can you be so tiresome! You must know that I am thinking of his marrying one of them.'

'Is that his design in settling here?'

'Design! Nonsense, how can you talk so! But it is very likely that he may fall in love with one of them, and therefore you must visit him as soon as he comes.'

'I see no occasion for that. You and the girls may go, or you may send them by themselves, which perhaps will be still better, for as you are as handsome as any of them, Mr Bingley might like you the best of the party.'

'My dear, you flatter me. I certainly have had my share of beauty, but I do not pretend to be any thing extraordinary now. When a woman has five grown up daughters, she ought to give over thinking of her own beauty.'

'In such cases, a woman has not often much beauty to think of.'

'But, my dear, you must indeed go and see Mr Bingley when he comes into the neighbourhood.'

'It is more than I engage for, I assure you.'

'But consider your daughters. Only think what an establishment it would be for one of them. Sir William and Lady Lucas are determined to go, merely on account, for in general you know they visit no new comers. Indeed you must go, for it will be impossible for us to visit him, if you do not.'

'You are over scrupulous surely. I dare say Mr Bingley will be very glad to see you; and I will send a few lines by you to assure him of my hearty consent to his marrying which ever he chuses of the girls; though I must throw in a good word for my little Lizzy.'

'I desire you will do no such thing. Lizzy is not a bit better than the others; and I am sure she is not half so handsome as Jane, or half so good humoured as Lydia. But you are always giving her the preference.'

'They have none of them much to recommend them,' replied he; 'they are all silly and ignorant like other girls; but Lizzy has something more of quickness than her sisters.'

'Mr Bennet, how can you abuse your own children in such a way? You take delight in vexing me. You have no compassion on my poor nerves.'

'You mistake me, my dear. I have a high respect for your nerves. They are my old friends. I have heard you mention them with consideration these twenty years at least.'

'Ah! you do not know what I suffer.'

'But I hope you will get over it, and live to see many young men of four thousand a year come into the neighbourhood.'

'It will be no use to us, if twenty such should come since you will not visit them.'

'Depend upon it, my dear, that when there are twenty, I will visit them all.'

Mr Bennet was so odd a mixture of quick parts, sarcastic humour, reserve, and caprice, that the experience of three and twenty years had been insufficient to make his wife understand his character. Her mind was less difficult to develope. She was a woman of mean understanding, little information, and uncertain temper. When she was discontent she fancied herself nervous. The business of her life was to get her daughters married; its solace was visiting and news.

Lesson Notes

Seated

Answer the following questions:
- Do you think that Mr and Mrs Bennet have different attitudes to the news of a young man arriving in the area?
- What is Mrs Bennet most excited about?
- How would you describe Mr Bennet's reaction?
- Look for ways in which Mr Bennet gently makes fun of his wife.
- Is Mrs Bennet aware of her husband's mockery?

Transform this chapter into a script. Underline the words spoken by Mrs Bennet in one colour and the words spoken by Mr Bennet in a different colour. You will notice that the reader is given no description of the setting. Decide where you think this action is located. Pencil in stage directions which make reference to:
- Tone of voice
- Reaction to what has been said
- Facial expression
- Movement

Active

Using the script you have just created, act out the scene between Mr and Mrs Bennet.

Written

Imagine that you are a servant who has been listening at the door. Later, while you are at the market, you report what you have heard to a servant from a different house. Write this as a script. Often when stories are repeated, things get exaggerated or embellished. Remember that overhearing such a conversation would give one servant superiority over another. This could also lead to details being exaggerated for effect.

Consider how these phrases might be changed and exaggerated in order to impress:
- *A young man of large fortune*
- *From the north of England*

- *He came down on Monday in a chaise and four*
- *Four or five thousand a year*
- *I will send a few lines by you to assure him of my hearty consent to his marrying whichever he chuses of the girls.*
- *…live to see many young men of four thousand a year come into the neighbourhood… I will visit them all.*

This written exercise should focus directly on the dialogue and therefore does not need stage directions.

Chapter Nineteen

The next day opened a new scene at Longbourn. Mr Collins made his declaration in form. Having resolved to do it without loss of time, as his leave of absence extended only to the following Saturday, and having no feelings of diffidence to make it distressing to himself even at the moment, he set about it in a very orderly manner, with all the observances which he supposed a regular part of the business. On finding Mrs Bennet, Elizabeth, and one of the younger girls together, soon after breakfast, he addressed the mother in these words,

'May I hope, Madam, for your interest with your fair daughter Elizabeth, when I solicit for the honour of a private audience with her in the course of this morning?'

Before Elizabeth had time for any thing but a blush of surprise, Mrs Bennet instantly answered.

'Oh dear! – Yes – certainly. – I am sure Lizzy will be very happy – I am sure she can have no objection. – Come Kitty, I want you up stairs.' And gathering her work together, she was hastening away, when Elizabeth called out,

'Dear Ma'am, do not go. – I beg you will not go. – Mr Collins must excuse me. – He can have nothing to say to me that any body need not hear. I am going away myself.'

'No, no, nonsense, Lizzy. – I desire you will stay where you are.' – And upon Elizabeth's seeming really, with vexed and embarrassed looks, about to escape, she added, 'Lizzy, I *insist* upon your staying and hearing Mr Collins.'

Elizabeth would not oppose such an injunction – and a moment's consideration making her so sensible that it would be wisest to get it over as soon and as quietly as possible, she sat down again, and tried to conceal by incessant employment the feelings which were divided between distress and diversion. Mrs Bennet and Kitty walked off, and as soon as they were gone Mr Collins began.

'Believe me, my dear Miss Elizabeth, that your modesty, so far from doing you any disservice, rather adds to your other perfections. You would have been less amiable in my eyes had there *not* been this little unwillingness; but allow me to assure you that I have your respected mother's permission for this address. You can hardly doubt the purport of my discourse, however your natural delicacy may lead you to dissemble; my attentions have been too marked to be mistaken. Almost as soon as I entered the house I singled you out as the companion of my future life. But before I am run away with by my feelings on this subject, perhaps it would be advisable to state my reasons for marrying – and moreover for coming into Hertfordshire with the design of selecting a wife, as I certainly did.'

The idea of Mr Collins, with all his solemn composure, being run away with by his feelings, made Elizabeth so near laughing that she could not use the short pause he allowed in any attempt to stop him farther, and he continued:

'My reasons for marrying are, first, that I think it a right thing for every clergyman in easy circumstances (like myself) to set the example of matrimony in his parish. Secondly, that I am convinced it will add very greatly to my happiness; and thirdly — which perhaps I ought to have mentioned earlier, that it is the particular advice and recommendation of the very noble lady whom I have the honour of calling patroness. Twice has she condescended to give me her opinion (unasked too!) on this subject; and it was but the very Saturday night before I left Hunsford — between our pools at quadrille, while Mrs Jenkinson was arranging Miss de Borough's foot-stool, that she said, "Mr Collins, you must marry. A clergyman like you must marry. — Chuse properly, chuse a gentlewoman for *my* sake; and for your *own*, let her be an active, useful sort of person, not brought up high, but able to make a small income go a good way. This is my advice. Find such a woman as soon as you can, bring her to Hunsford, and I will visit her." Allow me, by the way, to observe, my fair cousin, that I do not reckon the notice and kindness of Lady Catherine de Bourgh as among the least of the advantages in my power to offer. You will find her manners beyond any thing I can describe; and your wit and vivacity I think must be acceptable to her, especially when tempered with the silence and respect which her rank will inevitably excite. Thus much for my general intention in favour of matrimony; it remains to be told why my views were directed to Longbourn instead of my own neighbourhood, where I assure you there are many amiable young women. But the fact is, that being, as I am, to inherit this estate after the death of your honoured father, (who, however, may live many years longer), I could not satisfy myself without resolving to chuse a wife from among his daughters, that the loss to them might be as little as possible, when the melancholy event takes place — which, however, as I have already said, may not be for several years. This has been my motive, my fair cousin, and I flatter myself it will not sink me in your esteem. And now nothing remains for me but to assure you in the most animated language of the violence of my affection. To fortune I am perfectly indifferent, and shall make no demand of that nature on your father, since I am well aware that it could not be complied with; and that one thousand pounds in the 4 per cents. which will not be yours till after your mother's decease, is all that you may ever be entitled to. On that head, therefore, I shall be uniformly silent; and you may assure yourself that no ungenerous reproach shall ever pass my lips when we are married.'

It was absolutely necessary to interrupt him now.

'You are too hasty, Sir,' she cried. 'You forget that I have made no answer. Let me do it without farther loss of time. Accept my thanks for the compliment you are paying me. I am very sensible of the honour of your proposals, but it is impossible for me to do otherwise than decline them.'

'I am not now to learn,' replied Mr Collins, with a formal wave of the hand, 'that it is usual with young ladies to reject the addresses of the man whom they secretly mean to accept, when he first applies for their favour; and that sometimes the refusal is repeated a second or even a third time. I am therefore by no means discouraged by what you have just said, and shall hope to lead you to the alter ere long.'

'Upon my word, Sir,' cried Elizabeth, 'your hope is rather an extraordinary one after my declaration. I do assure you that I am not one of those young ladies (if such young ladies there are) who are so daring as to risk their happiness on the chance of being asked a second time. I am perfectly serious in my refusal. – You could not make me happy, and I am convinced that I am the last woman in the world who would make you so. – Nay, were your friend Lady Catherine to know me, I am persuaded she would find me in every respect ill qualified for the situation.'

'Were it certain that Lady Catherine would think so,' said Mr Collins very gravely – 'but I cannot imagine that her ladyship would at all disapprove of you. And you may be certain that when I have the honour of seeing her again I shall speak in the highest terms of your modesty, economy, and other amiable qualifications.'

'Indeed, Mr Collins, all praise of me will be unnecessary. You must give me leave to judge for myself, and pay me the compliment of believing what I say. I wish you very happy and very rich, and by refusing your hand, do all in my power to prevent your being otherwise. In making me the offer, you must have satisfied the delicacy of your feelings with regard to my family, and may take possession of Longbourn estate whenever it falls, without any self-reproach. This matter may be considered, therefore, as finally settled.' And rising as she thus spoke, she would have quitted the room, had not Mr Collins thus addressed her.

'When I do myself the honour of speaking to you next in this subject I shall hope to receive a more favourable answer than you have now given me; though I am far from accusing you of cruelty at present, because I know it to be the established custom of your sex to reject a man on the first application, and perhaps you have even now said as much to encourage my suit as would be consistent with the true delicacy of the female character.'

'Really, Mr Collins,' cried Elizabeth with some warmth, 'you puzzle me exceedingly. If what I have hitherto said can appear to you in the form of encouragement, I know not how to express my refusal in such a way as may convince you of its being one.'

'You must give me leave to flatter myself, my dear cousin, that your refusal of my address is merely words of course. My reasons for believing it are briefly these: – It does not appear to me that my hand is unworthy of your acceptance, or that the establishment I can offer would be any other than highly desirable. My situation in life, my connections with the family of De Bourgh, and my relationship to your own, are circumstances highly in my favour; and you should take it into farther consideration that in spite of your manifold attractions, it is by no means certain that another offer of marriage may ever be made you. Your portion is unhappily so small that it will in all likelihood undo the effects of your loveliness and amiable qualifications. As I must therefore conclude that you are not serious in your rejection of me, I shall chuse to attribute it to your wish of increasing my love by suspense, according to the usual practice of elegant females.'

'I do assure you, Sir, that I have no pretension whatever to that kind of elegance which consists in tormenting a respectable man. I would rather be paid the compliment of being believed. I thank you again and again for the honour you have done me in your proposals, but to accept them is absolutely impossible. My feelings in every respect forbid it. Can I speak plainer? Do not consider me now as an elegant female intending to plague you, but as a rational creature speaking the truth from her heart.'

'You are uniformly charming!' cried he, with an air of awkward gallantry; 'and I am persuaded that when sanctioned by the express authority of both your excellent parents, my proposals will not fail of being acceptable.'

To such perseverance in willful self-deception Elizabeth would make no reply, and immediately and in silence withdrew; determined, if he persisted in considering her repeated refusals as flattering encouragement, to apply to her father, whose negative might be uttered in such a manner as must be decisive, and whose behaviour at least could not be mistaken for the affectation and coquetry of an elegant female.

Chapter Twenty

Mr Collins was not left long to the silent contemplation of his successful love; for Mrs Bennet, having dawdled about in the vestibule to watch for the end of the conference, no sooner saw Elizabeth open the door and with quick step pass her towards the staircase, than she entered the breakfast-room, and congratulated both him and herself in warm terms on the happy prospect of their nearer connection. Mr Collins received and returned these felicitations with equal pleasure, and then proceeded to relate the particulars of the interview, with the result of which he trusted he had every reason to be satisfied, since the refusal which his cousin had steadfastly given him would naturally flow from her bashful modesty and the genuine delicacy of her character.

This information, however, startled Mrs Bennet; – she would have been glad to be equally satisfied that her daughter had meant to encourage him by protesting against his proposals, but she dared not to believe it, and could not help saying so.

'But depend on it, Mr Collins,' she added, 'that Lizzy shall be brought to reason. I will speak to her about it myself directly. She is a very headstrong foolish girl, and does not know her own interest; but I will *make* her know it.'

'Pardon me for interrupting you, Madam,' cried Mr Collins; 'but if she is really headstrong and foolish, I know not whether she would altogether be a very desirable wife to a man in my situation, who naturally looks for happiness in the marriage state. If therefore she actually persists in rejecting my suit, perhaps it would be better not to force her into accepting me, because if liable to such defects of temper, she could not contribute much to my felicity.'

'Sir, you quite misunderstood me,' said Mrs Bennet, alarmed. 'Lizzy is only headstrong in such matters as these. In every thing else she is as good natured a girl as ever lived. I will go directly to Mr Bennet, and we shall very soon settle it with her, I am sure.'

She would not give him time to reply, but hurrying instantly to her husband, called out as she entered the library,

'Oh! Mr Bennet, you are wanted immediately; we are all in an uproar. You must come and make Lizzy marry Mr Collins, for she vows she will not have him, and if you do not make haste he will change his mind and not have *her*.'

Mr Bennet raised his eyes from his book as she entered, and fixed them on her face with a calm unconcern which was not in the least altered by her communication.

'I have not had the pleasure of understanding you,' said he, when she had finished her speech. 'Of what are you talking?'

'Of Mr Collins and Lizzy. Lizzy declares she will not have Mr Collins, and Mr Collins begins to say that he will not have Lizzy.'

'And what am I to do on the occasion? – It seems an hopeless business?'

'Speak to Lizzy about it yourself. Tell her that you insist upon her marrying him.'

'Let her be called down. She shall hear my opinion.'

Mrs Bennet rang the bell, and Miss Elizabeth was summoned to the library.

'Come here, child,' cried her father as she appeared. 'I have sent for you on an affair of importance. I understand that Mr Collins has made you an offer of marriage. Is it true?' Elizabeth replied that it was. 'Very well – and this offer of marriage you have refused?'

'I have, Sir.'

'Very well. We now come to the point. Your mother insists upon your accepting it. Is it not so, Mrs Bennet?'

'Yes, or I will never see her again.'

'An unhappy alternative is before you, Elizabeth. From this day you must be a stranger to one of your parents. – Your mother will never see you again if you do *not* marry Mr Collins, and I will never see you again if you *do*.'

Elizabeth could not but smile at such a conclusion of such a beginning; but Mrs Bennet, who had persuaded herself that her husband regarded the affair as she wished, was excessively disappointed.

'What do you mean, Mr Bennet, by talking in this way. You promised me to insist upon her marrying him.'

'My dear,' replied her husband, 'I have two small favours to request. First, that you will allow me the free use of my understanding on the present occasion; and secondly, of my room. I shall be glad to have the library to myself as soon as may be.'

Not yet, however, in spite of her disappointment in her husband, did Mrs Bennet give up the point. She talked to Elizabeth again and again; coaxed and threatened her by turns. She endeavoured to secure Jane in her interests, but Jane with all possible mildness declined interfering; – and Elizabeth sometimes with real earnestness and sometimes with playful gaiety replied to her attacks. Though her manner varied however, her determination never did.

Lesson Notes

Seated

In pairs

Consider the long speech made by Mr Collins beginning *My reasons for marrying are...* and ending *...when we are married.*

Pencil a ring around all the full stops in this speech. What do you notice about the length of the sentences?

There are only four very short sentences. Which ones are they and what effect do they have in contrast to the others?

Hot-seat the following:

One of you will be in role as Elizabeth, the other will be the interviewer who asks her to speak aloud the thoughts going through her head in reaction to Mr Collins' speech. Choose five individual moments from his speech and think about what questions Elizabeth might have asked herself at this point.

Active

Punctuation walk

A large, clear space will be needed for this activity.

Everyone in the class will walk around the room reading Mr Collins' speech aloud. Change the direction you are walking in at every punctuation mark.

Written

Using the skills developed in your work on chapter one of *Pride and Prejudice*, turn the prose into a script. Use the descriptions between the dialogue to help you with appropriate stage directions.

Begin with, *Sir you quite misunderstand me,* and end with *...was excessively disappointed.*

Create a storyboard for the key events in chapter twenty.

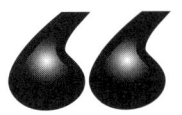

Lady Windermere's Fan

Lady Windermere's Fan was written by Oscar Wilde in 1892. It is a comedy that demonstrates Wilde's flair for humorous and witty dialogue.

The play was presented to Victorian theatre-goers who would, themselves, have been rich, privileged and aristocratic or upper class and the audience would have recognised the characters in this play as belonging to the same society as themselves. The aristocratic characters in *Lady Windermere's Fan* were extremely concerned with high social status, good manners, etiquette, making a good and well-connected marriage and avoiding scandal. People judged each other almost entirely by appearance, wealth and social connection.

This extract is from the opening scene. The audience has already been introduced to the main character: Lady Windermere, on the afternoon of her 'coming of age' (her 21st birthday). She is visited at home by Lord Darlington, who flirts with her and, inexplicably to her, claims that if a husband is unfaithful to his wife, the wife should claim the right to behave in the same way herself. Lady Windermere is taken aback and shocked. Immediately afterwards, Parker, the butler announces the arrival of the Duchess of Berwick and her daughter.

Characters
Lady Windermere
Lord Darlington
The butler, Parker
Duchess of Berwick
Lady Agatha Carlisle

Act One, Scene One

Parker:	The Duchess of Berwick and Lady Agatha Carlisle.
	Enter the Duchess of Berwick and Lady Agatha Carlisle. Exit Parker.
Duchess of Berwick:	(*approaches and shakes hands*) Dear Margaret, I am so pleased to see you. You remember Agatha, don't you? (*crosses to Lord Darlington*) How do you do, Lord Darlington? I won't let you know my daughter, you are far too wicked.
Lord Darlington:	Don't say that, Duchess. As a wicked man I am a complete failure. Why, there are lots of people who say I have never really done anything wrong in the whole course of my life. Of course

they only say it behind my back.

Duchess of Berwick: Isn't he dreadful? Agatha, this is Lord Darlington. Mind you don't believe a word he says. No, no tea, thank you, dear. (*crosses and sits on sofa*) We have just had tea at Lady Markby's. Such bad tea, too. It was quite undrinkable. I wasn't at all surprised. Her own son-in-law supplies it. Agatha is looking forward so much to your ball tonight, dear Margaret.

Lady Windermere: (*seated*) Oh, you mustn't think it is going to be a ball, Duchess. It is only a dance in honour of my birthday. A small and early.

Lord Darlington: (*standing*) Very small, very early, and very select, Duchess.

Duchess of Berwick: (*on sofa*) Of course it's going to be select. But we know that, dear Margaret, about your house. It is really one of the few houses in London where I can take Agatha, and where I feel perfectly secure about dear Berwick. I don't know what society is coming to. The most dreadful people seem to go everywhere. They certainly come to my parties – the men get quite furious if one doesn't ask them. Really, some one should make a stand against it.

Lady Windermere: I will, Duchess. I will have no one in my house about whom there is any scandal.

Lord Darlington: Oh, don't say that, Lady Windermere. I should never be admitted! (*sitting*)

Duchess of Berwick: Oh, men don't matter. With women it is different. We're good. Some of us are, at least. But we are positively getting elbowed into the corner. Our husbands would really forget our existence if we didn't nag them from time to time, just to remind them that we have a perfect legal right to do so.

Lord Darlington: It's a curious thing, Duchess, about the game of marriage – a game, by the way, that is going out of fashion – the wives hold all the honours, and invariably lose the odd trick.

Duchess of Berwick: The odd trick? Is that the husband, Lord Darlington?

Lord Darlington: It would be rather a good name for the modern husband.

Duchess of Berwick:. Dear Lord Darlington, how thoroughly depraved you are!

Lady Windermere: Lord Darlington is trivial.

Lord Darlington: Ah, don't say that, Lady Windermere.

Lady Windermere: Why do you talk so trivially about life, then?

Lord Darlington: Because I think that life is far too important a thing ever to talk seriously about it.

Duchess of Berwick: What does he mean? Do, as a concession to my poor wits, Lord Darlington, just explain to me what you really mean.

Lord Darlington: (*stands*) I think I had better not, Duchess. Nowadays to be intelligible is to be found out. Goodbye! (*shakes hands with Duchess*) And now – (*goes up stage*) Lady Windermere, goodbye. I may come tonight, mayn't I? Do let me come.

Lady Windermere: (*standing up stage with* Lord Darlington) Yes, certainly. But you are not to say foolish, insincere things to people.

Lord Darlington: (*smiling*) Ah! you are beginning to reform me. It is a dangerous thing to reform any one, Lady Windermere. (*bows and exits*).

Duchess of Berwick: (*rising*) What a charming, wicked creature. I like him so much. I'm quite delighted he's gone! How sweet you're looking! Where do you get your gowns? And now I must tell you how sorry I am for you, dear Margaret. (*crosses to sofa and sits with* Lady Windermere) Agatha, darling!

Lady Agatha: Yes, Mamma (*rises*).

Duchess of Berwick: Will you go and look over the photograph album that I see there?

Lady Agatha: Yes, Mamma (*goes to table*).

Duchess of Berwick: Dear girl! She is so fond of photographs of Switzerland. Such a pure taste, I think. But I really am so sorry for you, Margaret.

Lady Windermere: (*smiling*) Why, Duchess?

Duchess of Berwick: Oh, on account of that horrid woman. She dresses so well, too, which makes it much worse, sets such a dreadful example. Augustus – you know my disreputable brother – such a trial to us all – well, Augustus is completely infatuated about her. It is quite scandalous, for she is absolutely inadmissible into society. Many a woman has a past, but I am told that she has at least a dozen, and that they all fit.

Lady Windermere: Whom are you talking about, Duchess?

Duchess of Berwick: About Mrs Erlynne.

Lady Windermere: Mrs Erlynne? I never heard of her, Duchess. And what has she to do with me?

Duchess of Berwick: My poor child! Agatha, darling!

Lady Agatha: Yes, mamma.

Duchess of Berwick: Will you go out on the terrace and look at the sunset?

Lady Agatha: Yes, mamma (*exits through window*).

Duchess of Berwick: Sweet girl! So devoted to sunsets! Shows such refinement of feeling, does it not? After all, there is nothing like Nature, is there?

Lady Windermere: But what is it, Duchess? Why do you talk to me about this person?

Duchess of Berwick:. Don't you really know? I assure you we're all so distressed about it. Only last night at dear Lady Jansen's every one was saying how extraordinary it was that, of all men in London, Windermere should behave in such a way.

Lady Windermere: My husband – what has he got to do with any woman of that kind?

Duchess of Berwick: Ah, what indeed, dear? That is the point. He goes to see her continually, and stops for hours at a time, and while he is there she is not at home to any one. Not that many ladies call on her, dear, but she has a great many disreputable men friends – my own brother particularly, as I told you – and that is what makes it so dreadful about Windermere. We looked upon *him* as being such a model husband, but I am afraid there is no doubt about it. My dear nieces – you know the Saville girls, don't you? – such nice domestic creatures – plain, dreadfully plain, but so good – well, they're always at the window doing fancy work, and making ugly things for the poor, which I think so useful of them in these dreadful socialistic days, and this terrible woman has taken a house in Curzon Street, right opposite them – such a respectable street, too! I don't know what we're coming to! And they tell me that Windermere goes there four and five times a week – they see him. They can't help it – and although they never talk scandal, they – well, of course – they remark on it to every one. And the worst of it all is that I have been told that this woman has got a great deal of money out of somebody, for it seems that she came to London six months ago without anything at all to speak of, and now she has this charming house in Mayfair, drives her ponies in the Park every afternoon and all – well, all – since she has known poor dear Windermere.

Lady Windermere: Oh, I can't believe it!

Duchess of Berwick: But it's quite true, my dear. The whole of London knows it. That is why I felt it was better to come and talk to you, and advise you to take Windermere away at once to Homburg or to Aix, where he'll have something to amuse him, and where you can watch him all day long. I assure you, my dear, that on several occasions after I was first married, I had to pretend to be very ill, and was obliged to drink the most unpleasant mineral waters, merely to get Berwick out of town. He was so extremely susceptible. Though I am bound to say he never gave away any large sums of money to anybody. He is far too high-principled for that!

Lady Windermere: (*interrupting*) Duchess, Duchess, it's impossible! (*rises and crosses room*) We are only married two years. Our child is but six months old (*sits in chair*).

Duchess of Berwick: Ah, the dear pretty baby! How is the little darling? Is it a boy or a girl? I hope a girl – Ah, no, I remember it's a boy! I'm so sorry. Boys are so wicked. My boy is excessively immoral. You wouldn't believe at what hours he comes home. And he's only left Oxford a few months – I really don't know what they teach them there.

Lady Windermere: Are *all* men bad?

Duchess of Berwick: Oh, all of them, my dear, all of them, without any exception. And they never grow any better. Men become old, but they never become good.

Lady Windermere: Windermere and I married for love.

Duchess of Berwick: Yes, we begin like that. It was only Berwick's brutal and incessant threats of suicide that made me accept him at all, and before the year was out, he was running after all kinds of petticoats, every colour, every shape, every material. In fact, before the honeymoon was over, I caught him winking at my maid, a most pretty, respectable girl. I dismissed her at once without a character. – No, I remember I passed her on to my sister; poor dear Sir George is so short-sighted, I thought it wouldn't matter. But it did, though – it was most unfortunate. (*rises*) And now, my dear child, I must go, as we are dining out. And mind you don't take this little aberration of Windermere's too much to heart. Just take him abroad, and he'll come back to you all right.

Lady Windermere: Come back to me?

Duchess of Berwick: Yes, dear, these wicked women get our husbands away from us, but they always come back, slightly damaged, of course. And don't make scenes, men hate them!

Lady Windermere: It is very kind of you, Duchess, to come and tell me all this. But I can't believe that my husband is untrue to me.

Duchess of Berwick: Pretty child! I was like that once. Now I know that all men are monsters (*Lady Windermere rings bell*). The only thing to do is to feed the wretches well. A good cook does wonder, and that I know you have. My dear Margaret, you are not going to cry?

Lady Windermere: You needn't be afraid, Duchess, I never cry.

Duchess of Berwick: That's quite right, dear. Crying is the refuge of plain women but the ruin of pretty ones. Agatha, darling.

Lady Agatha: (*entering*) Yes, mamma.

Duchess of Berwick: Come and bid goodbye to Lady Windermere, and thank her for your charming visit. And by the way, I must thank you for sending a card to Mr Hopper – he's that rich young Australian people are taking such notice of just at present. His father made a great fortune by selling some kind of food in circular tins – most palatable, I believe – I fancy it is the thing the servants always refuse to eat. But the son is quite interesting. I think he's attracted by dear Agatha's clever talk. Of course, we should be very sorry to lose her, but I think that a mother who doesn't part with a daughter every season has no real affection. We're coming tonight, dear. (*Parker opens doors*) And remember my advice, take the poor fellow out of town at once, it is the only thing to do. Goodbye, once more; come, Agatha.

Exit Duchess and Lady Agatha.

Lady Windermere: How horrible! I understand now what Lord Darlington meant by the imaginary insistence of the couple not two years married. Oh! It can't be true – she spoke of enormous sums of money paid to this woman. I know where Arthur keeps his bank book – in one of the drawers of that desk. I might find out by that. I *will* find out.

Lesson Notes

Seated

In pairs

Read the conversation between Lady Windermere and the Duchess of Berwick, from the exit of Lord Darlington to the end.

Read it through aloud once and discuss what you have noticed about each character. You should comment on the huge enjoyment that the Duchess obviously gets from delivering bad news and how important she obviously feels herself to be. She enjoys this position of power. Lady Windermere has the disadvantage of age, knowledge and experience in this situation and can only protest her disbelief.

Now read the text aloud again, but this time, stop after each character's speech and discuss what thoughts you think are really going through the characters' minds – think about the difference between what is actually said (the text) and what is being thought (the sub-text). For example, in the Duchess of Berwick's first speech, when she says, 'How sweet you're looking,' she is likely to be thinking something along the lines of: 'You're such an innocent young thing with not a care in the world. Let's change that! Let's see you crumble!' And when Lady Windermere replies, (smiling) 'Why, Duchess?' she is likely to be thinking, 'Keep smiling, don't let her see that she's got to you!'

Active

In pairs

You will have noticed how much the Duchess enjoys taking the moral high ground in this situation with Lady Windermere. Indeed, she treats her in a very childlike way. The Duchess is obviously a gossip at heart, who relishes the power of delivering bad news and the higher status this gives her.

In pairs, look at the following lines and for each one, devise a freeze-frame snapshot with both of you in character. You should think carefully about how to arrange yourselves in each freeze-frame so as to show the high /low status. Consider facial expression, body language, reaction, use of height (standing up gives instant status).

- *Duchess: Dear girl!...*
  Lady W: Why, Duchess?
- *Duchess: Oh, on account of that horrid woman...*
  Lady W: Whom are you talking about, Duchess?
- *Duchess: Don't you really know?...*
  Lady W: My husband – what has he...?
- *Lady W: Oh, I can't believe it!*
  Duchess: But it's quite true my dear...
- *Lady W: Are all men bad?*
  Duchess: Oh, all of them...
- *Lady W: Windermere and I married for love.*
  Duchess: Yes, we begin like that...
- *Lady W: It is very kind of you...*
  Duchess: Pretty child!...

Written

As far as the plot of *Lady Windermere's Fan* goes, it is not unlike a storyline from a soap opera. The audience discovers in Act 2 that Mrs Erlynne is, in fact Lady Windermere's mother, who abandoned her husband and child twenty years earlier for another man. In the meantime, however, Lady Windermere has become so convinced that her husband and Mrs Erlynne are having an affair that she decides to punish him by eloping with Lord Darlington. Mrs Erlynne discovers this plan and is determined to save her daughter from repeating her own disastrous mistake. Eventually, she does, although she (temporarily) ruins her own reputation in doing so. In the end, she does not reveal herself to Lady Windermere as her mother, but is content to have saved her daughter from ruin.

Write two scenes from a present day soap opera in script format, using the following plot guides:

● Scene 1
Plot: the boyfriend/husband or girlfriend/wife of the main character is suspected of two-timing with someone else. A gossip takes great pleasure in informing her/his friend of what is assumed to be happening. The main character is at first, totally disbelieving but is gradually persuaded that this may be the truth.

● Scene 2
Plot: (some time later) It is discovered that, in fact, the 'other' man/woman is the mother/father of the main character, who abandoned the main character as a baby. What happens next?

Macbeth

Macbeth was written by William Shakespeare around 1605-1606, and was one of his greatest tragedies. It is a play about kingship and a traitor who overthrows the rightful ruler of his country.

In the scene below, Macbeth, a brave soldier, returns to his wife after killing Duncan, the king of his country. Macbeth had been persuaded to murder the king by his wife, Lady Macbeth. She planned the murder after learning that three witches had foretold that Macbeth would become king of Scotland. Macbeth has the opportunity to commit the murder because King Duncan is staying in Macbeth's castle. At the beginning of this scene, Lady Macbeth tells the audience that she has drugged Duncan's bodyguards.

Act Two, Scene Two

Inverness. Macbeth's castle. Enter Lady Macbeth.

Lady Macbeth: That which hath made them drunk hath made me bold;
What hath quench'd them hath given me fire. Hark!
Peace!
It was the owl that shriek'd, the fatal bellman,
Which gives the stern'st good-night. He is about it.
The doors are open; and the surfeited grooms
Do mock their charge with snores. I have drugg'd their possets,
That death and nature do contend about them,
Whether they live or die.

Macbeth: (*within*) Who's there! What, ho!

Lady Macbeth: Alack! I am afraid they have awak'd,
And 'tis not done. Th' attempt, and not the deed,
Confounds us. Hark! I laid their daggers ready;
He could not miss 'em. Had he not resembled
My father as he slept, I had done't.

Enter Macbeth.

My husband!

Macbeth: I have done the deed. Didst thou not hear a noise?

Lady Macbeth: I heard the owl scream and the crickets cry.
Did not you speak?

Macbeth: When?

Lady Macbeth: Now.

Macbeth: As I descended?

Lady Macbeth: Ay.

Macbeth: Hark!
Who lies i' the second chamber?

Lady Macbeth: Donalbain.

Macbeth: (*looking on his hands*) This is a sorry sight.

Lady Macbeth: A foolish thought to say a sorry sight.

Macbeth: There's one did laugh in's sleep, and one cried 'Murder!'
That they did wake each other. I stood and heard them;
But they did say their prayers, and address'd them
Again to sleep.

Lady Macbeth: There are two lodg'd together.

Macbeth: One cried 'God bless us,' and 'Amen' the other,
As they had seen me with these hangman's hands.
List'ning their fear, I could not say 'Amen'
When they did say 'God bless us!'

Lady Macbeth: Consider it not so deeply.

Macbeth: But wherefore could not I pronounce 'Amen'?
I had most need of blessing, and 'Amen'
Stuck in my throat.

Lady Macbeth: These deeds must not be thought
After these ways: so, it will make us mad.

Macbeth: Methought I heard a voice cry 'Sleep no more;
Macbeth does murder sleep' – the innocent sleep,
Sleep that knits up the ravell'd sleave of care,
The death of each day's life, sore labour's bath,
Balm of hurt minds, great nature's second course,
Chief nourisher in life's feast.

Lady Macbeth: What do you mean?

Macbeth: Still it cried 'Sleep no more' to all the house;
'Glamis hath murder'd sleep; and therefore Cawdor
Shall sleep no more – Macbeth shall sleep no more'.

Lady Macbeth: Who was it that thus cried? Why, worthy Thane,
You do unbend your noble strength to think
So brainsickly of things. Go get some water
And wash this filthy witness from your hand.
Why did you bring these daggers from the place?
They must lie there. Go carry them, and smear
The sleepy grooms with blood.

Macbeth: I'll go no more:
I am afraid to think what I have done;
Look on't again I dare not.

Lady Macbeth: Infirm of purpose!
Give me the daggers. The sleeping and the dead
Are but as pictures; 'tis the eye of childhood
That fears a painted devil. If he do bleed,
I'll gild the faces of the grooms withal,
For it must seem their guilt.

Exit. Knocking within.

Macbeth: Whence is that knocking?
How is't with me, when every noise appals me?
What hands are here? Ha! they pluck out mine eyes.
Will all great Neptune's ocean wash this blood
Clean from my hand? No; this my hand will rather
The multitudinous seas incarnadine,
Making the green one red.

Re-enter Lady Macbeth.

Lady Macbeth: My hands are of your colour; but I shame
To wear a heart so white. (K*nock*) I hear a knocking
At the south entry; retire we to our chamber.
A little water clears us of this deed.
How easy it is then! Your constancy
Hath left you unattended. (K*nock*) Hark! more knocking.
Get on your nightgown, lest occasion call us
And show us to be watchers. Be not lost
So poorly in your thoughts.

Macbeth: To know my deed, 'twere best not know myself. (K*nock*)
Wake Duncan with thy knocking? I would thou couldst!

Exeunt.

Lesson Notes

Seated

In pairs

The murder of King Duncan is not shown. Instead, Macbeth describes what happened in the chamber.

- List three advantages and three disadvantages of this dramatic technique.
- Do you have any ideas why Shakespeare decided to stage this moment in this way?
- If you were directing a modern performance of *Macbeth*, how would you choose to stage this particular scene? Remember that the atmosphere should convey fear, anxiety, tension and horror. Give ideas about how colour and lighting could be best used to make the audience feel involved.
- Underline words associated with the following senses: sight, touch, sound and smell. Make suggestions about the effect that these words would have on the audience's imagination.

Active

In groups

In a group of six, while Macbeth describes what happened when he murdered Duncan, mime the scene of Duncan's death. Begin with the line, *Macbeth: (within) Who's there! What, ho!*

You will need the following characters to read aloud from the script:
- Macbeth
- Lady Macbeth

And four further characters to enact the mime:
- The two people sleeping outside Duncan's chamber (note that we are not told who they are – they could be Malcolm and Donalbain or two guards).
- Duncan
- Macbeth

In pairs

This activity is about showing whether a character feels powerful or weak. A powerful state can be shown by turning and facing the other character and maintaining eye contact. A weak state of mind is shown by turning away from the other character and not being able to look at him/her.

Act out each of the following pairs of lines, deciding which character feels powerful and which character feels weak.

- *Macbeth:*   Who's there? What, ho!
  Lady Macbeth: Alack! I am afraid they have awak'd...

- *Macbeth:*   This is a sorry sight.
  Lady Macbeth: A foolish thought to say a sorry sight.

- *Lady Macbeth:*   These deeds must not be thought
  After these ways: so, it will make us mad.

Macbeth:	Methought I heard a voice cry 'Sleep no more; Macbeth does murder sleep'…
● *Lady Macbeth:*	Why did you bring these daggers from the place? They must lie there. Go carry them, and smear The sleepy grooms with blood.
Macbeth:	I'll go no more: I am afraid to think what I have done; Look on't again, I dare not.

What have you noticed about who is the strongest in this scene? Are you surprised that Macbeth reacts in this way?

Written

Using your ideas from the activities above, write out director's notes for actors who are playing this scene. Consider the following:
- spacing
- eye-contact
- tone of voice
- use of props (particularly the daggers)
- pace

Pay careful attention to directing the actor playing Macbeth, in telling him how to show the change from being a strong soldier to being weak and afraid.

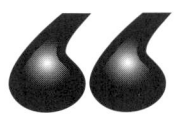

Macbeth

Towards the end of the play, Lady Macbeth's gentlewoman has called upon a doctor to observe Lady Macbeth sleepwalking. In the following scene the audience sees a dramatic change in Lady Macbeth and, in her sleep, she reveals that there is more than the murder of Duncan on her mind: she talks of Banquo (one of Macbeth's friends, murdered by men hired by Macbeth) and the wife of the Thane of Fife (killed with her children by Macbeth's men).

Act Five, Scene One

Dunsinane. Macbeth's castle. Enter a doctor of physic and a waiting-gentlewoman.

Doctor: I have two nights watch'd with you, but can perceive no truth in your report. When was it she last walk'd?

Gentlewoman: Since his Majesty went into the field, I have seen her rise from her bed, throw her nightgown upon her, unlock her closet, take forth paper, fold it, write upon't, read it, afterwards seal it, and again return to bed; yet all this while in a most fast sleep.

Doctor: A great perturbation in nature, to receive at once the benefit of sleep and do the effects of watching! In this slumb'ry agitation, besides her walking and other actual performances, what, at any time, have you heard her say?

Gentlewoman: That, sir, which I will not report after her.

Doctor: You may to me; and 'tis most meet you should.

Gentlewoman: Neither to you nor any one, having no witness to confirm my speech.

Enter Lady Macbeth with a taper.

Lo you, here she comes! This is her very guise; and, upon my life, fast asleep. Observe her; stand close.

Doctor: How came she by that light?

Gentlewoman: Why, it stood by her. She has light by her continually; 'tis her command.

Doctor: You see her eyes are open.

Gentlewoman: Ay, but their sense is shut.

Doctor: What is it she does now? Look how she rubs her hands.

Gentlewoman: It is an accustomed action with her, to seem thus washing her hands; I have know her continue in this a quarter of an hour.

Lady Macbeth: Yet here's a spot.

Doctor:	Hark, she speaks. I will set down what comes from her, to satisfy my remembrance the more strongly.
Lady Macbeth:	Out, damned spot! Out, I say! One, two; why then 'tis time to do't. Hell is murky. Fie, my lord, fie! A soldier, and afeard? What need we fear who knows it, when none can call our pow'r to account? Yet who would have thought the old man to have had so much blood in him?
Doctor:	Do you mark that?
Lady Macbeth:	The Thane of Fife had a wife; where is she now? What, will these hands ne'er be clean? No more o' that, my lord, no more o' that; you mar all with this starting.
Doctor:	Go to, go to; you have known what you should not.
Gentlewoman:	She has spoke what she should not, I am sure of that. Heaven knows what she has known.
Lady Macbeth:	Here's the smell of the blood still. All the perfumes of Arabia will not sweeten this little hand. Oh, oh, oh!
Doctor:	What a sigh is there! The heart is sorely charg'd.
Gentlewoman:	I would not have such a heart in my bosom for the dignity of the whole body.
Doctor:	Well, well, well.
Gentlewoman:	Pray God it be, sir.
Doctor:	This disease is beyond my practice. Yet I have known those which have walk'd in their sleep who have died holily in their beds.
Lady Macbeth:	Wash your hands, put on your nightgown, look not so pale. I tell you yet again, Banquo's buried; he cannot come out on's grave.
Doctor:	Even so?
Lady Macbeth:	To bed, to bed; there's knocking at the gate. Come, come, come, come, give me your hand. What's done cannot be undone. To bed, to bed, to bed.
	Lady Macbeth exits.
Doctor:	Will she go now to bed?
Gentlewoman:	Directly.
Doctor:	Foul whisp'rings are abroad. Unnatural deeds Do breed unnatural troubles; infected minds To their deaf pillows will discharge their secrets. More needs she the divine than the physician. God, God forgive us all. Look after her; Remove from her the means of all annoyance, And still keep eyes upon her. So, good night. My mind she has mated, and amaz'd my sight. I think, but dare not speak.
Gentlewoman:	Good night, good doctor.
	Exeunt.

Lesson Notes

Seated

Look for comparisons between Act Five, Scene One and Act Two, Scene Two. Consider character changes and recurring imagery.

Active

In groups

In groups of five, one person should be Lady Macbeth and the others should act as a chorus. You can take it in turns to be Lady Macbeth.

Lady Macbeth speaks the first line and the chorus echoes her with the second.

Lady Macbeth's lines are from Act Five, Scene One and the lines spoken by the chorus are taken from what Lady Macbeth said in Act Two, Scene Two. You will notice that the lines from Act Two act as an echo.

Lady Macbeth:	Out, damned spot! Out, I say!
Chorus:	Go get some water
	And wash this filthy witness from your hand.
Lady Macbeth:	Yet who would have thought the old man to have had so much blood in him?
Chorus:	The sleeping and the dead
	Are but as pictures; 'tis the eye of childhood
	That fears a painted devil.
Lady Macbeth:	What, will these hands ne'er be clean?
Chorus:	My hands are of your colour; but I shame
	To wear a heart so white.
Lady Macbeth:	Here's the smell of the blood still; all the perfumes of Arabia will not sweeten this little hand.
Chorus:	A little water clears us of this deed.
	How easy is it then!

During your performance, experiment with the following techniques:
Using space
● circle around Lady Macbeth holding hands
● stand behind Lady Macbeth
● space yourselves in four corners of a square with Lady Macbeth in the centre
● move in on Lady Macbeth, invading her personal space.

Using your voice
● whispering/hissing
● varying the volume, one loud followed by one soft
● chanting/sing-song/mocking tone
● making it sound eerie – try to emphasise vowel sounds (e.g. Thaaane).

You may wish to repeat each pair of lines in order to create more impact.

Written

Lady Macbeth's gentlewoman tells the doctor that she has seen Lady Macbeth 'take forth paper, fold it, write upon't, read it, afterwards seal it'. What do you think she is writing?

Write this document as if you were Lady Macbeth.

Notes

Other drama material available from Evans

STAR PLAYS
by Keith west

Six short plays for large casts, ideal for reading aloud in KS3 and KS4 English/drama lessons, offering two science fiction plays, two teenage adventures and two dramatised versions of classic novels.

GRAPHIC SHAKESPEARE
By Hilary Burningham

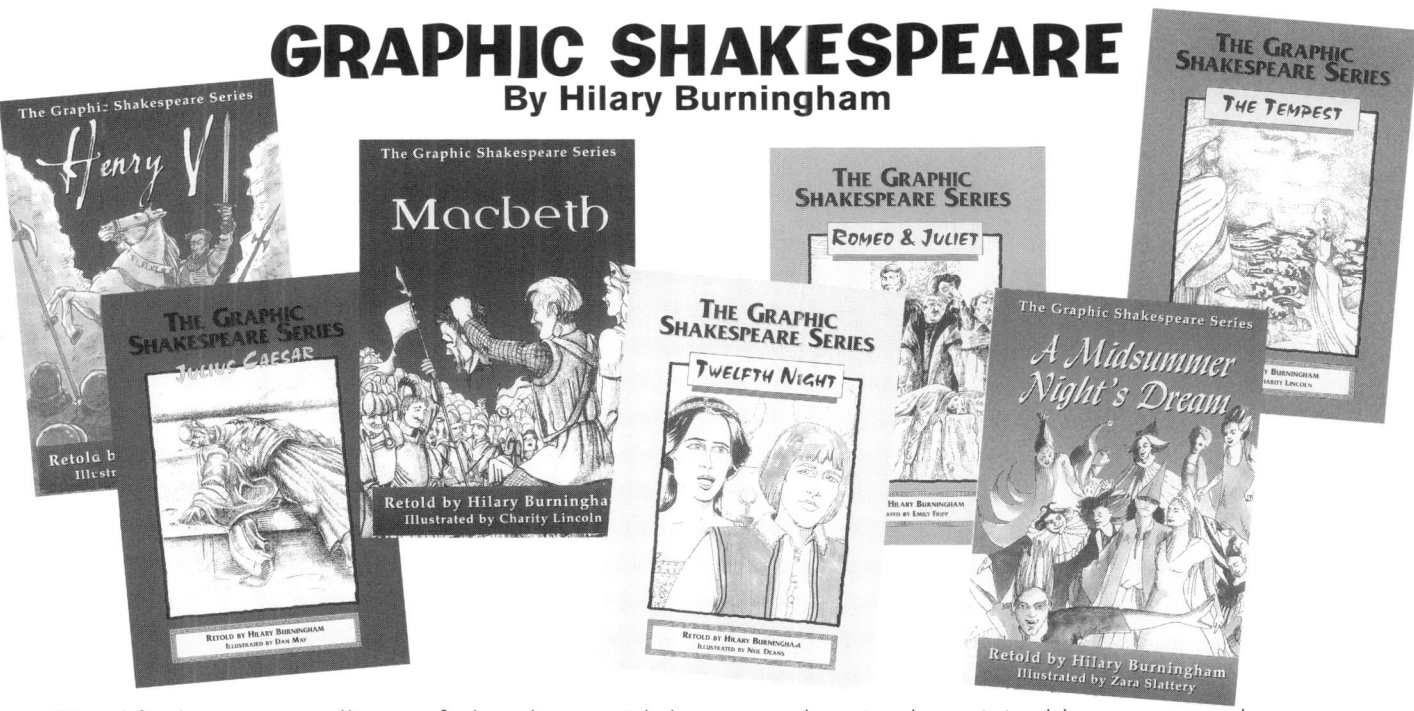

Simplified prose retellings of the plays, with key speeches in the original language and dramatic illustrations. Perfect for introducing younger students to Shakespeare's work, as study aids for students with special educational needs and as revision tools.

To find out more, or to order, please contact Evans Brothers Ltd, telephone 020 7487 0920, or visit www.evansbooks.co.uk